RELIVING VATICAN II

RELIVING VATICAN II

IT'S ALL ABOUT JESUS CHRIST

CARDINAL JUSTIN RIGALI

LTP

LITURGY
TRAINING
PUBLICATIONS

RELIVING VATICAN II: IT'S ALL ABOUT JESUS CHRIST © 2006 Archdiocese of Chicago: Liturgy Training Publications, 1800 North Hermitage Avenue, Chicago IL 60622; 1-800-933-1800, fax 1-800-933-7094, e-mail orders@ltp.org. All rights reserved. See our website at www.LTP.org.

Cover photo © 2005 JAT

Printed in the United States of America.

Library of Congress Control Number: 2005936776

ISBN-10: 1-56854-597-5
ISBN-13: 978-1-56854-597-4

REVAT

Dedication

This work is prayerfully dedicated
to His Holiness Pope Benedict XVI.
As the present Successor of Peter
and Vicar of Christ for the universal Church,
and as Guarantor of the faithful continuity
of the 2,000-year-old Tradition of the Church,
he has begun his pontificate by confirming
his determination to continue to implement
the Second Vatican Council.

Table of Contents

Foreword

Almost two generations have passed since Vatican II, and we are beginning to be able to grasp the wisdom of historical perspectives, to revisit, rediscover, and relive Vatican II.

Our fast-moving world presents to us wonderful opportunities to receive complete and accurate information, but also the daunting challenge of encountering partial or filtered facts. The documents of the Second Vatican Council are no exception.

The documents have brilliantly described the Truth and Love of Jesus Christ for His Church, and everyone has the privilege and right to be enriched by this Truth and Love.

Vatican II has been a great gift of the Holy Spirit to the Church, to the world, and to each of us. It is a treasure for us all. We cannot allow it to remain a buried treasure on the bottom of the sea of current challenges.

The following reflections were originally presented on the Eternal Word Television Network. I hope that in this printed and slightly modified form they will help people to relive Vatican II, above all its concentration on the person of Jesus Christ.

The detailed Table of Contents may help us enter into the content of this great gift of the Holy Spirit.

+Justin Card. Rigali

Introduction

The subject of these reflections is the Second Vatican Council, what it meant for the Church and what it still means for the Church. I wish to speak about its content, its message, what it said and what it did not say. I am absolutely convinced that the Second Vatican Council was a great grace for the Church and for the world. It has involved an extraordinary outpouring of the Holy Spirit in the Church in our day.

I was privileged to be present at Vatican II everyday during the first two sessions of 1962 and 1963. This event influenced my life and I am happy to share my observations with whoever will find these useful. Vatican II was the twenty-first Ecumenical Council in the life of the Church. It meant *continuity* with all of the Councils that preceded it. Pope Benedict XVI inaugurated his pontificate, pledging its continued implementation.

The Council was a great opportunity for the Church to *concentrate above all on Jesus Christ, His Gospel, His Church.*

To Speak about Jesus

Permit me to share with you an experience I had a number of years ago in Rome. I think that when you hear it, you will agree that it is relevant to what Vatican II was all about. I had the opportunity one day to be present in the Vatican with Mother Teresa of Calcutta. Mother Teresa had been honored with an international award, and the Holy See wished to draw attention to her or rather to her work. With this intention, the Vatican organized a gathering of ambassadors from different countries to listen to Mother Teresa's presentation. Before the ceremony, at which the Pope was present, I had the opportunity to ask Mother Teresa what she would be speaking about. Her response was intriguing. She smiled and then she said to me: "Oh, I don't know. All I know is that I will be speaking about Jesus."

And that, it seems to me, is what Vatican II endeavored to do—*to speak about Jesus.* Since the light of Jesus Christ shines in His Church, the message of the Council is about *the Church of Jesus Christ* and the Gospel of Jesus Christ, which the Church is charged to preach. But the Gospel and the Church are all about the person of Jesus Christ.

Everything that Vatican II did was to present Jesus Christ and His teaching to the world, to make Jesus Christ accessible in His Church.

The history of Vatican II is linked to God's merciful plan to pour out His Holy Spirit in a new Pentecost of the twentieth century.

On October 28, 1958, Angelo Giuseppe Roncalli, Patriarch of Venice, was elected to succeed Pius XII as Pope. He was seventy-six years of age, actually one month short of seventy-seven. He qualified to be called, in the words of Saint John: "A man sent by God whose name was John."

To Renew Our Faith and Promote Holiness

Three months after his election Pope John XXIII startled the world on January 25, 1959, with an announcement that he made in the Basilica of Saint Paul's outside the Walls. In this magnificent Basilica where the Apostle to the Nations is buried, John XXIII announced his intention *to call an Ecumenical Council,* the twenty-first in the history of the

Church and in the history of the world. He asked the world
to pray.

Then, on December 25, 1961, after almost two years
of preparation, John XXIII told the world that the Council
would open the following year, in 1962. In this document,
dated Christmas Day, Pope John XXIII gave us so many
insights into what he wanted this Ecumenical Council *to be*
and *to do*.

His first remark on this occasion was one of confidence in Jesus Christ, invoking His promise in the Gospel:
"Behold I am with you all days, even to the end of the
world" (Matthew 28:20). Pope John listed different aspects
of the forthcoming Council through which the Church
desired to renew her faith, to reflect on her unity, to promote
the sanctification of her members, the diffusion of divine
truth, and the consolidation of her structures. In other words,
he was talking about faith, unity, holiness, truth, and
renewal. This was *the real agenda of Vatican II*.

In its efforts to rebuild the visible unity of all
Christians, the Council should, in the thought of Pope
John, more fruitfully present *the doctrine of the Church* and
show signs of *fraternal charity* in the world. Pope John asked
all the members of the Church to offer prayers for the success of the Council. Then came that beautiful invitation
to all Christians separated from the Catholic Church to pray
that the Council might be advantageous also for them.

Finally there was the prayer of Pope John: "Renew
your wonders in our time as though through a new Pentecost,
and grant that the holy Church, persevering unanimously
and fervently in prayer, together with Mary, the Mother of
Jesus and also under the guidance of Blessed Peter may
build up the Kingdom of the divine Savior, a kingdom of
truth and justice, a kingdom of love and peace. Amen."

All this was the proximate vision of Pope John for the Council that would begin in less than ten months. This was the vision, the mood, the sentiments that Pope John hoped to instill into the Church. These were his expectations of Vatican II and he wanted to share them with the Church and with the world.

A Solemn Day for the Whole World

Finally the day came, October 11, 1962. In the liturgical calendar of those years, October 11 was the feast of the Maternity of Mary, the Mother of God. I was privileged to be in Rome at that time, as a student priest, and I was privileged to have the opportunity to serve as one of the priest assistants at the Council. At the beginning of Vatican II, general concelebration of the Eucharist in the Latin Church was not permitted. In order to facilitate the presence of priests at the opening of the Council, Pope John had authorized the priests of Rome to offer Masses at midnight, in preparation for the Council. In those years, midnight Mass was generally reserved for Christmas and the Easter vigil.

In the early morning of October 11, 1962, it poured rain in Rome, but all of a sudden the sun came out and twenty-five hundred Bishops were able to process through St. Peter's Square into St. Peter's Basilica. As one of the priest assistants, I too was able to join the procession.

Last in line was Pope John XXIII who, according to the custom of that day, was carried in on the sedia gestatoria, a portable chair. Being elevated in this way, he was able to be seen more easily by the people in the Square. His face was serene as usual, but also solemn. He exuded *confidence*. His voice, which was part of the great charism of his person, was deep and paternal, inspiring *trust*. In the Basilica, besides the Bishops of the Church, there were observers, Catholics and separated brethren; there were also representatives of various categories of the people of God.

From Every Corner of the World

For the first time in the history of the world such a vast number of Bishops were gathered with the Successor of Peter in offering the Sacrifice of the Mass. The Bishops were spread out through the entire nave of the Basilica, reaching to the back. Bishops came from every corner of the world. The mission lands were well represented. So were the Eastern Rites. There were some Bishops from the Communist world, including those of Poland. Among these was a young Bishop who sat toward the back of the Basilica, the Auxiliary Bishop of Krakow, Karol Wojtyla. A number of Bishops were conspicuously absent, those who were in prison, those who were suffering for the faith and were impeded by tyrannical regimes from being present. This extraordinary convocation of Bishops, some twenty-five hundred, was in sharp contrast to the much smaller group of Bishops that had been present in 1870 at the previous Ecumenical Council, which was Vatican I. The First Vatican Council had not needed the nave of the Basilica and it utilized only the transepts. There was no comparison between the universal representation of the Church at the First Vatican Council of 1870 and that of the Second Vatican Council in 1962. I still wonder how I could ever have been so fortunate as to be present for this event.

In his address to the Council, Pope John began: "Mother Church rejoices . . . under the auspices of the Virgin Mother of God." And he concluded by solemnly proclaiming Jesus Christ: "To Jesus Christ our most loving Redeemer, immortal King of peoples and of times, be Love, Power, and Glory for ever and ever."

And, in between the beginning and the end of his address, the Pope sketched *the principal aim of the Second Vatican Council* and how it was to be attained. These words of his guided the Council, but must continue to guide the postconciliar period for years yet to come: "The principal aim—he said—of the Ecumenical Council is this: that the sacred deposit of Christian doctrine should be more effectively guarded and taught."

So much of the Council was about the Church's teaching, about doctrine, about truth—the Truth incarnate in Jesus Christ. Pope John was explicit, saying that the Ecumenical Council "wishes to transmit the doctrine, pure and integral, without any attenuation or distortion, which throughout twenty centuries, not withstanding difficulties and contrasts, has been the common patrimony of mankind." Then he added: "From the renewed, serene and tranquil adherence to all the teaching of the Church in its entirety and preciseness, as it still shines forth in the Acts of the Council of Trent and the First Vatican Council, the Christian, Catholic and apostolic spirit of the entire world expects a step forward toward a doctrinal penetration and a formation of consciousness in faithful and perfect conformity to the authentic doctrine."

Pope John then highlighted an important principle: "The substance of the ancient doctrine of the deposit of faith is one thing, and the way in which it is presented is another." And that is what he had in mind when he stated: "The principal aim of the Ecumenical Council is this: that the sacred deposit of Christian doctrine should be more effectively guarded and taught." The substance of the doctrine was immutable, but under the inspiration of the Holy Spirit the teaching could and should indeed be more effectively presented or taught.

To Present the Truth with the Medicine of Mercy

Over and over again the Pope stressed the need for the Church's doctrine. The Church was to open the fountain of her life-giving doctrine. This is the way Vatican II intended to react to error, not with the severity, Pope John said, of condemnations, but with *the medicine of mercy* that would exalt truth.

In this initial address, the Pope also showed *his passion for unity:* "First, unity in the Church. And then, unity with those Christians separated from the Church. And then, unity with all mankind."

All of this was part of Pope John's vision of the Council that he would inaugurate, but not conclude. That would be left to his great successor Pope Paul VI.

Another dimension of the Council's inauguration took place that night. Rome was gloriously illuminated. The Pope came to his window in the Apostolic Palace to greet the crowds that awaited him in St. Peter's Square. Then came his famous speech. Even the moon, he said, was rejoicing that night! And then, with his characteristic ability to endear himself to so many, he spoke to the parents. He encouraged them to go home and caress their children and tell them that this embrace came from the Pope!

The people of Rome and far beyond cannot forget that night. They cannot forget those words. They cannot forget the smile and the love of Papa Giovanni, *il Papa buono,* the good and kind Pope who personally reflected so much of the love of Jesus Christ which he was urging the Church to live and to communicate.

It all made sense to good Pope John, because he was applying the principle he had enunciated that morning: "To Jesus Christ our most loving Redeemer, immortal King of peoples and of times, be Love, Power and Glory forever and ever."

And so Vatican II began to be a reality for the Church and for the world. It was to be all about *Jesus Christ* and *His Church and His Gospel,* and *how we are to live together in truth and love.*

On that first day no one could foresee everything that would take place. But Vatican II could already say what Mother Teresa would say some years later: "All I know is that I will be speaking about Jesus."

I

The Church:
The Light of the Nations

Reflection on *the Church of Jesus Christ* was to be the corner-stone of the entire Second Vatican Council. This is so, precisely because the light of Jesus Christ shines in His Church, and precisely because Jesus Christ is present in His Church. The Church belongs to Jesus Christ. She is His Church.

I remember on one occasion, during the pontificate of Pope Paul VI, how he offered a reflection on Saint Matthew's Gospel, the sixteenth chapter. He quoted the encounter of Peter with Jesus, how Peter said to Jesus: "You are the Christ, the Son of the living God." And then Pope Paul quoted Jesus' response to Peter: "You are Peter and upon this rock I will build my Church."

In citing that verse from the Gospel of Saint Matthew, the Holy Father chose to emphasize a particular word. He read the passage this way: "You are Peter and upon this rock I will build *my* Church." The Pope went on to explain that, in serving the Church, he, as Pope, was given special prerogatives, a special role of power to be used as service. He realized that as the Successor of Peter, he was endowed with full and supreme power in the Church.

Belonging to Jesus Christ

He went on, however, to explain that this power of service, which was vested in him, was given him *only for a season.*

The Church belongs to Jesus Christ and to Him alone. "You are Peter and upon this rock I will build my Church." And what Pope Paul said about himself and his role in the Church, as being only for a season, applies to all of us who have the great blessing of serving the Church. It is *only for a season.* Christ never gives up the governance of His Church. He never gives the Church exclusively to anyone. Even the Vicar of Christ for the universal Church, the Successor of Peter, governs the Church only for a season. The Church is uniquely related to Christ. Christ possesses her as His own.

In the thought of the Fathers of the Second Vatican Council, by reason of her relationship with Christ, the Church is called *a kind of sacrament of intimate union with God and of the unity of all mankind.* The Church is a sign, an instrument that belongs to Christ. And by this instrument, Christ unites people with God and brings all mankind to unity.

Vatican II set out to explain the nature and the mission of the Church. The Council mentioned how in God's plan all those who would believe in Christ were to be assembled in the community of the Church. Jesus, the Son of the living God, had been sent on a mission by His Father, a mission of salvation. And at Pentecost, the Holy Spirit was sent as Jesus had been sent, so that Jesus' mission would continue in the Church. The result is that the Church is described as a people made one with the unity of the Father, the Son, and the Holy Spirit.

The Dogmatic Constitution on the Church, which is called *Lumen Gentium,* "The Light of the Nations," is divided into eight chapters. We could reflect on the content of all eight of these chapters for hours and hours. The main divisions, however, of the document are these: 1) the Mystery of the Church; 2) the People of God; 3) the Hierarchical

Structure of the Church; 4) the Laity; 5) the Call to Holiness; 6) Religious; 7) the Eschatological State of the Church; and 8) Mary, the Mother of God.

The Mystery of the Church: A Divine Reality with Many Dimensions

In chapter one, the Council presented the Church as *a mystery*. By that, the Council meant a divine reality with many facets. The content of the mystery of the Church is so rich that it must be expressed through many comparisons. And this is what is done in the Sacred Scriptures. There are many different figures that are used to describe the Church in her totality.

The Church is looked upon as a *sheepfold* whose door is Christ. Another comparison is the Church as a *flock* whose shepherd is God. The Church is compared to *a tract of land that is the field of God* and on which grows an ancient olive tree onto which the Gentiles have been engrafted. The Church is a *vineyard*. The Church is explained by Jesus Himself by the allegory of *the vine and the branches*. He says explicitly, "I am the vine, you are the branches."

The Church is considered *the edifice, the building of God* that has the Lord Jesus as its cornerstone. The Church is *the house of God, His family, the household of God, His dwelling place*. The Church is *a temple* of God made up of living stones. It is called *the Jerusalem that is above*. The Church, in the expression of Saint Paul, is *our Mother*. She is spoken of as a *spotless spouse* of the spotless Lamb. The Church is loved and cherished by Christ, joined to Him, and subject to Him in love and fidelity.

Another comparison is the human body in which there are different members. The Church is described as *the

Body of Christ, because Christ is the Head and we are the members. The Church is described as *the Bride of Christ,* because she is loved by Christ with spousal love. The Church is looked to as *the pillar and mainstay of truth.* It is the Church handed over to Peter to be shepherded—the one, holy, Catholic, and apostolic Church, one Church in her holy charisms and her external organization.

The Church is also a Church that embraces sinners, and at the same time she is always in need of being purified. Incessantly she pursues the path of penance and renewal. The Church has always gloried in her penitents and among them are Peter and Paul, and Mary Magdalene. The Church, Saint Augustine will tell us, is like a pilgrim in a foreign land, pressing forward amid the persecutions of the world and the consolations of God. In all of these comparisons, the Second Vatican Council endeavored to present the Church as *a mystery of love coming forth from the Most Blessed Trinity.*

The People of God Called into Being by Christ

The second chapter is devoted to *the People of God.* It is this image that the Church dwelled upon in great detail. In this chapter, we find a very important principle that says: "It has pleased God to make people holy and to save them, not merely as individuals without any mutual bonds, but by making them into a single people" (no. 9), which is a single body, the Church. In the Old Testament there was a covenant between God and His people that foreshadowed the New Covenant instituted by His Blood (cf. 1 Corinthians 11:25).

By His Death and Resurrection Christ called into being a new people. Christ is the Head of His people who are called to dignity and freedom through the Blood of Jesus that is applied through Baptism. The people of God make up the initial stage of the Kingdom of God. The Church is meant for all regions of the earth. The Second Vatican Council tells us that *the people of God exist in order to take part in the Eucharistic Sacrifice,* which is the source and summit of the entire Christian life. Already in this document, the Council speaks to us of the Church in relationship to the sacraments. It speaks of Baptism, Confirmation, the Eucharist, and Penance, in which we receive pardon from the mercy of God. It speaks to us of the Anointing of the Sick, Holy Orders, and Matrimony, which brings forth a family, which is the domestic Church.

The whole people of God share the priestly and prophetic office of Jesus Christ. The Council explains to us that there is an essential distinction between the priesthood of the laity and the ministerial priesthood. The entire people of God are called to be prophetic, to bear witness to the Gospel. And the people of God preserve the faith from generation to generation with the assistance of the Holy Spirit, being anointed as they are by the Holy One.

The Second Vatican Council brings out forcefully the dignity of the whole body of the Church, which in effect is, in its overwhelming proportion, laypeople. But every member has the privilege of being part of the people of God *by reason of Baptism.* Already in the Constitution on the Church we have an indication of the Church's attitude on ecumenism. Our relationship with separated Christians is through the Sacred Scripture, through faith in the Trinity, through Baptism; with some it is also through an acceptance of the Episcopacy and the Eucharist; with some through the acceptance of marriage as a sacrament. All hold prayer as a common gift. Already the document on the Church speaks of the relationship with non-Christians and gives a primacy of place to the Jewish people by reason of their election by God. Our Muslim brothers and sisters are mentioned with respect, and it is made very clear that all those who strive for salvation will not be deprived of God's gift. The people of God also have the obligation of spreading the faith.

In the Hierarchical Structure: The Sacred Power of Service

The genius of Vatican II's presentation of the Church is that it starts from *the mystery of the Church and the People of God.* And then, in subsequent chapters, we have a breakdown of what makes up the people of God—the various categories. And so, in chapter three, we have *the hierarchical structure* of the Church, made up of Bishops, priests, and deacons, to all of whom is given a sacred power of service— service for the benefit of the entire body. Here we find the will of God spelled out, how Jesus sent His Apostles as He had been sent by His Father. Here we find the doctrine that Peter has been placed over the other Apostles. The Council teaches that the Bishops are the Successors of the Apostles and that they govern the Church, together with the Successor of Peter, who is recognized as the Vicar of Christ and the visible head of the whole Church.

We are reminded that, in the choice of Apostles, Jesus chose those whom He wanted, and this mission was to last for all times. In this chapter we see the special spiritual role of Bishops and find here a favorite text of Pope John Paul II: "In the Bishops, therefore, whom the priests assist, the Lord Jesus Christ, the Supreme High Priest, is present in the midst of those who believe" (no. 21).

The Council presents this magnificent insight into *the role of the Bishop, who with His priests is a sign of Jesus*

Christ in the midst of the Church. The Bishop, like Christ, is the good shepherd. The sacramentality of the episcopate is asserted by Vatican II. Consecration confers the office of sanctifying, teaching and governing. The doctrine of collegiality is embraced by the Council. Just as the Apostles were joined in a college, so the Bishops today, with the Roman Pontiff, constitute the Episcopal College, and this College is the subject of full, supreme, and universal power in the Church. At the same time, the Pope alone is the Vicar of Christ for the universal Church, and as Pastor of the whole Church has full, supreme, and universal power. The individual Bishop is the Vicar of Christ in his diocese and must promote and safeguard the unity of faith and the discipline common to the whole Church. He must teach love for the whole Mystical Body of Christ. Among the principal duties of the Bishop, the proclamation of the Gospel has an eminent place. The highest form of proclamation is the sacramental proclamation of the Eucharist, in which the Death and Resurrection of the Lord are proclaimed sacramentally.

Contained in the hierarchical structure of the people of God and at the service of the entire people of God we have the *priests* who are sharers with the Bishop in the shepherd's role. Vatican II tells us that priests exercise the function of Christ above all in the Eucharist. They are related to the Bishops as brothers, sons, friends, and co-workers. And they gather together in the unity of the presbyterate, closely united with the Bishop.

The *deacon* is portrayed as one engaged in liturgy, in the ministry of the word and in charity, as well as administration. The Second Vatican Council envisioned the possibility of restoring the permanent diaconate and recommended it to the Pope. Subsequently, Paul VI acted on this suggestion and for many years now we have the restored diaconate in the life of the Church.

Chapter four presents *the laity*. Later on we will consider the laity in a special document of the Council on the lay apostolate. But here Vatican II enunciates the magnificent principle: "Bishops know that they were not meant by Christ to shoulder alone the entire saving mission of the Church" (no. 30). The lay apostolate is a participation in the very saving mission of the Church. Through Baptism and Confirmation all of her members are commissioned to the apostolate by the Lord Himself. By their activities the laypeople have the special role of consecrating the world itself to God.

Universal Call to Holiness—Religious—Pilgrim Church

Chapter five presents *the universal call to holiness*. No category in the Church is excluded from this privilege and from this obligation. Bishops, priests, deacons, married couples, parents, widows, single people, workers, the oppressed—everyone is called to the fullness of Christian life through Baptism.

Chapter six deals with *consecrated religious*. The deep insight into the meaning of religious life is found in these words of *Lumen Gentium:* "Although the religious state constituted by the profession of the evangelical counsels does not belong to the hierarchical structure of the Church, nevertheless it belongs inseparably to her life and holiness" (no. 44). What a beautiful tribute to millions of religious. We think of the religious we know—the Sisters and Brothers who taught in our schools, worked in our hospitals, the missionary Sisters, Brothers, and priests who have gone all

over the world to witness to holiness and to proclaim
the Gospel.

I had the privilege to be assigned, as a young priest,
to the service of the Holy See on the island of Madagascar.
I remember how deeply edified I was to visit a cemetery
where missionaries were buried—the missionaries who had
come, sent by the Church and by Christ, with the commitment to proclaim the Gospel. They came to Madagascar
and to so many other countries to live and to die there. And
their memory is blessed in the Church.

The *eschatological nature of the pilgrim Church* and her
union with the heavenly Church is presented in chapter
seven. Here the Church renews her faith in *heaven*. Here
also the Church reminds us of the limitless mercy of God
that gives us the opportunity, even after death, of being
purified. And this is what the Church has always meant
by *purgatory*.

Mary, Mother of the Church and Our Mother

Chapter eight is devoted to *the Blessed Virgin Mary*. I remember, in the Council, the great solicitude of the Bishops to
show special honor to Mary. At one moment there were
two groups. The first group said: it is really important for us
to write a separate document on the Blessed Virgin Mary.
In this way, people will understand that we are serious
about showing Mary special honor. Her position in the
Church is special. We must avoid giving the impression
that Vatican II is downplaying Mary. A separate document
is the answer. The other group said *no*. If we are going
to promote true devotion to Mary, we must show her role
in relation to the Church. She is, after all, the Mother of
Christ and His Church. Any treatise on the Church would

be incomplete without Mary. A special chapter in the
Constitution on the Church would be better than
a separate document.

Two respectable opinions, two points of view that
do not deny the faith. The Council voted and there was a
slight majority, which the Pope accepted. This side favored
the inclusion of the treatise on the Blessed Virgin in the
document on the Church. And so today the last chapter of
the Constitution on the Church deals with Mary.

It is called "The Blessed Virgin Mary, Mother of
God, in the Mystery of Christ and the Church." The document shows Mary's role of collaboration in God's plan of
salvation. It shows her relationship to the Church. It points
out the maternal love with which Mary cares for us—the
brothers and sisters of Jesus. It confirmed the beautiful
titles whereby Mary is invoked as *Advocate, our Help, our
Mediatrix.* In all of this, the Council expressed the lofty
yet subordinate role of Mary to Her Son Jesus, the one
Mediator with the Father. Her divine maternity is clearly
recognized, as is her maternity in our regard.

During the Council, Pope Paul VI wanted to honor
Mary with another explicit title: *Mother of the Church.*
Today there is an altar in St. Peter's Basilica that bears this
inscription. Pope John Paul II added an image of Mary
that is visible in St. Peter's Square. It too honors Mary as
Mother of the Church.

The Second Vatican Council will always be remembered as a Council that, in continuity with the other
Councils in the Church's life, not only honored Mary,
but also highlighted her relationship to the Church.
She is the Mother of the Church, the type of the Church,
the Model of the Church, the one who already possesses
the holiness to which all members of the Church are called.

With the treatise on Mary, the Council closes its reflection on the Church. How beautiful, since, with Mary, the Church's reflection on Jesus began, because in the fullness of time, God sent His Son born of a woman and the Word was made flesh. And the Mother of the Son, the Mother of the Word, is forever the Mother of His Church!

II

The Sacred Liturgy:
The Official Prayer of the Church

What was so impressive in the sessions of Vatican II was to see how the Book of the Gospels, the word of God, was enshrined in St. Peter's Basilica. It was the inspiration and center of all discussions. The first item on the Council's agenda was the question of the *renewal of the sacred liturgy*. The liturgical renewal in the Church had been going on for years, especially since the turn of the century. Pope Pius XII had given a great impetus to this revival in 1947, with the publication of his encyclical *Mediator Dei*. This document certainly had a great impact on Vatican II and its discussions on the sacred liturgy. Pius XII gave a great deal of credit for liturgical renewal to the Benedictine Order.

The results of the discussions on the liturgy became the law of the Church a whole year after the opening of the Council. On December 4, 1963, the Constitution on the Sacred Liturgy was signed by the new Pope, Paul VI, and by all the Bishops at the second session of the Council.

In the organization of the Second Vatican Council, the theme of the sacred liturgy was deliberately placed first, because of the importance of the topic and its relevance to the life of the Church.

When finally promulgated, the document bore the title of the first two words: *Sacrosanctum Concilium,* "the Sacred Council."

This document has certainly had an enormous impact on the Latin Church. We must keep in mind that the document does not change the Church's liturgy as it is celebrated in the Eastern rites.

Full, Conscious, and Active Participation

But what did this document say about the liturgy of the Church? What did it want the Latin Church to do? What did Vatican II want to do about the liturgy? Did it want the Church to abolish Latin in the Mass? Did it want the Blessed Sacrament removed from the main altar? Did it authorize concelebration? Did it eliminate Benediction of the Blessed Sacrament? Did it promote Holy Communion under both kinds? Did it want better participation in the Eucharistic Sacrifice?

The Constitution on the Sacred Liturgy wanted above all to set forth general principles—and some very important ones—about liturgical renewal and about promoting *full, conscious,* and *active* participation in the liturgy of the Church. In his 1947 encyclical on the liturgy, Pope Pius XII had strongly emphasized the importance of the people's zealous, active and deep participation.

The Council's document on the liturgy was written with the knowledge that its implementation would depend on the Holy See. There were many things that would need subsequent clarification, application and implementation. This process was carried on, first by Pope Paul VI and then by Pope John Paul II. Now it is in the hands of Pope Benedict XVI.

We all know that the liturgical renewal has had rocky moments in its application. Many things attributed to Vatican II are simply unauthorized interpretations of Vatican II or of the Holy See's subsequent implementation of Vatican II. But the document itself is *a great gift to the Church* and has made possible extremely important contributions to the liturgy and to the way we worship God.

The ongoing implementation of Vatican II requires— like everything delicate in the Church—fidelity to what the Church says and teaches, and a *profound sense of reverence* in the liturgy.

The document is divided into seven chapters and it is worthwhile to list them: 1) General Principles for the Renewal and Promotion of the Sacred Liturgy, 2) the Eucharistic Mystery, 3) the other Sacraments and Sacramentals, 4) the Divine Office, 5) the Liturgical Year, 6) Sacred Music, and 7) Sacred Art and Sacred Furnishings.

All of these topics are of great importance, but the first two need our special attention.

First of all, what are the principles that the Church wants us to understand and to follow in the question of true liturgical renewal?

But even before asking ourselves that question, we must have a clear idea of what the sacred liturgy is. What is its nature, its importance?

The Exercise of the Priesthood of Jesus Christ

Basically, the sacred liturgy is *the official prayer of the Church.* The Council tells us clearly that "the liturgy is considered the exercise of the priesthood of Jesus Christ" (no. 7). And how wonderful to realize that we are all associated in different ways in the exercise of Christ's priesthood! And again: "In the liturgy is exercised the full public worship by the Mystical Body of Jesus Christ, that is by the Head and his members" (no. 8). Because the liturgy is the official prayer of the Church, the Council goes on to say: "The liturgy is the summit toward which the action of the Church is directed and, at the same time, the source from which all her power flows" (no. 10). Another beautiful passage of Vatican II says that "the sacred Liturgy is principally the worship of the divine majesty" (no. 33). The Council challenges us to think what all of this means in the context of a congregation worshipping in our parishes on Sunday, or a vast crowd participating in the Eucharistic Sacrifice offered by the Holy Father in Rome, or a lone priest celebrating Mass secretly in a communist prison.

Once we understand the nature of the liturgy, the Council tells us that "it is necessary that the faithful come to it with proper dispositions. . . . Pastors of souls must therefore realize that, when the liturgy is celebrated, more is required than the mere observance of the laws governing valid and licit celebration. It is their duty also to ensure that the faithful take part *knowingly, actively* and *fruitfully*" (no. 11).

In another similar paragraph the Council says: "Mother Church earnestly desires that all the faithful be led to that *full, conscious* and *active* participation in liturgical celebrations which is demanded by the very nature of the liturgy" (no. 14). This participation is considered a right and duty of the faithful by reason of their Baptism. And, since *the liturgy is the primary and indispensable source from which the faithful derive the Christian spirit,* it follows that, in the renewal and promotion of the sacred liturgy, the aim to be considered before all else is *participation by all the faithful.*

This full and active, conscious and fruitful participation in the prayer of the Church and in the exercise of the priesthood of Christ is what Vatican II wanted and what the Church still wants today. And, if we return to the description of the sacred liturgy as being "principally *the worship of the divine majesty*" (no. 33), then we can easily understand why the Church wants us to participate fully and consciously, actively and fruitfully in this worship of the divine majesty.

But, in the concrete, what makes up the liturgy of the Church? The liturgy is first of all the Eucharistic Sacrifice, then the other Sacraments and the Divine Office.

Profound Reverence:
Internal-External, Individual-Communal

Any participation that is full and conscious, active and fruitful is certainly much more than external. We are talking about a participation that is profoundly *reverent*, that is, internal and *external*, a participation that is *individual* and *communal*. The liturgy that we celebrate is much more than *my* liturgy. It is Christ's liturgy and the liturgy of all our brothers and sisters. I must invest myself fully, in participating in the liturgy with all my fervor and with my mind and heart, but I cannot prescind from my fellow worshippers. In the liturgy, we worship together. There are times when we need to be alone with God, but the liturgy is not one of these private moments. Even in the sacred encounter of the Sacrament of Penance, we are not alone. We confess to the priest, as minister of the Church, acting in the name of Jesus Christ.

And, even if there are no other worshippers besides the priest or besides the priest and myself, the Eucharistic worship belongs to the whole Church. The Decree on the Priesthood tells us that "even if the faithful are unable to be present at Mass, it is an act of Christ and the Church" (*Presbyterorum Ordinis*, 13).

If we grasp the principle that the liturgy requires both individual and communal participation, then we can understand that there is a place in the liturgy for *silence*, for *singing*, and also for acknowledging and greeting our neighbor with the *sign of Christ's peace*. There are some communities that are very conscious of worshipping together. They realize the need to be united with their neighbor and everyone in the Church. And this is excellent. But the Church never intended that this togetherness be totally expressed at the sign of peace. Our communal worship presumes that we greet people as we arrive at church and as we leave. It presumes that we help one another all during the week, that we assist the poor and those in need, that we share the joys and sorrows of the members of the community. At the sign of peace, the Church requests us simply to exchange to those next to us the peace of Christ. This moment is not intended to excuse us from other contacts with our brothers and sisters. The sign of peace is meant to be a sign of Christ's peace, not an extended conversation.

The liturgy requires an equilibrium of worship. People's preferences differ. It is not up to the priest or any group of people to impose their preferences on the congregation. It is, however, necessary to take into account the common good. And the common good demands effort, mutual understanding, patience, sacrifice, and obedience to the Church's liturgical norms.

Main Principles

Apart from the supreme aim of liturgical renewal—the full and conscious, active and fruitful participation of the faithful in the liturgy—what are the other main principles that the Council sets forth? These are some:

- Regulation of the sacred liturgy depends on the authority of the Church; it is not left to individuals to change the liturgy, its components or its approved language (cf. no. 22).

- Sacred Scripture is of paramount importance in the celebration of the liturgy (cf. no. 25). The Council speaks of a double table: the table of God's word and the table of sacrifice. In other words, the altar and the ambo.

- Liturgical actions are not private functions but celebrations of the Church, which is "the sacrament of unity" (cf. no. 26).

- The communal celebration of the liturgy is generally to be preferred, when possible, to an individual and quasi-private celebration (cf. no. 27).

- In liturgical celebrations, whether as a minister or as one of the faithful, everyone should exclusively perform his or her own role (cf. no. 28).

- To promote active participation, the people should be encouraged to take part by means of acclamations, responses, psalms, antiphons, and songs, as well as by actions, gestures, and positions. At the proper time a sacred silence should be observed (cf. no. 30).

- In the liturgy God speaks to His people as Christ proclaims His Gospel. The people reply to God by song and by prayer (cf. no. 33).

- Preaching should draw its content mainly from scriptural and liturgical sources as a proclamation of the wonderful works of God in the history of salvation (cf. no. 35).

- As we all know, the use of the vernacular was authorized by Vatican II. This limited usage was later extended by the Holy See, but the use of Latin and of Latin hymns was not abolished. Its use is to be determined by pastoral criteria, of which the local Bishop is the judge (cf. no. 36).

- Any adaptations of the liturgy depend on the Holy See and proper episcopal authority (cf. nos. 22 and 36).

Among the principles for the renewal and promotion of the liturgy, Vatican II encourages the parishes to have *a sense of community,* above all in the common celebration of the Sunday Mass (cf. no. 42). A magnificent implementation of this directive was given by Pope John Paul II when he issued *Dies Domini.*

The Most Sacred Mystery: Sacrifice and Supper

In the second chapter of the Constitution on the Liturgy, the Church expresses her profound reverence for "the most sacred mystery of the Eucharist." The theology of the Church is beautifully summarized in no. 47: "At the Last Supper, on the night when he was betrayed, our Savior instituted the Eucharistic Sacrifice of his Body and Blood. He did this in order to perpetuate the sacrifice of the Cross throughout the centuries until he should come again, and so to entrust to his beloved spouse, the Church, a memorial of his death and resurrection: a sacrament of love, a sign of unity, a bond of charity, a paschal banquet in which Christ is consumed, the mind is filled with grace, and a pledge of future glory is given to us." In this expression of the Church's faith we see how aptly Vatican II teaches the Church's tradition about the Eucharist as Sacrifice and Supper, and as the memorial of Christ's death and resurrection. It makes so much sense then that Vatican II should desire that the faithful not be present at the Eucharist "as strangers or silent spectators" (no. 48).

In this same chapter Vatican II restored concelebration, limiting it to certain times. Subsequently, the Holy
See has made it possible in general. The importance of *the
homily* is stressed as being part of the liturgy itself. Greater
use of the Scriptures is provided for. Communion under
both kinds, subsequently confirmed for all Masses with the
Bishop's authorization, was permitted, while the dogmatic
principles of the Council of Trent were reiterated. The constant faith of the Church, however, is that *Christ is present
and received—body and blood, soul and divinity—under the
sign of bread or wine.* The reception of both consecrated
species, when possible, in the subsequent implementation
by the Holy See, is considered a fuller outward sign of
following Christ's command both to eat and drink. The
Council itself highly recommended that, when possible, the
faithful receive hosts consecrated at the same Mass. This
recommendation was nothing new. Pius XII had asked for
this in his encyclical Mediator Dei in 1947. This practice
emphasizes that Holy Communion is an intimate
participation in the Eucharistic Sacrifice.

In chapter four, the Divine Office is looked upon
as a means for the Church to continue Christ's priestly
work, to praise the Lord, and to intercede for the salvation
of the whole world.

In chapter five, Vatican II enunciates *the meaning
of the liturgical year.* As the Church recalls *the events or
mysteries of the redemption,* she opens up to the faithful the
riches of the power and merits of Christ, so that these are
in some way made present to the faithful who are enabled
to take hold of them and become filled with saving grace.
This beautiful teaching of the Council was anticipated by
decades in the writings of Blessed Columba Marmion, OSB,

who died in 1923. His work *Christ in His Mysteries* is a forerunner of this deep insight of Vatican II.

The dignity of sacred music and the role of sacred art and sacred furnishings have been diligently presented in the Constitution on the Liturgy. The validity of the important Catholic practice of honoring sacred images in churches has been reconfirmed. The Council also accepted the possibility of assigning the date of Easter to a fixed date if there is ecumenical support.

While presenting the great dignity of the liturgy, the Constitution on the Sacred Liturgy points out that the liturgy still does not exhaust the entire activity of the Church.

Popular piety is another aspect of Catholic life and it too has been affirmed by Vatican II. Some time ago the Congregation for Divine Worship and the Discipline of the Sacraments issued a directory on popular piety. Pope John Paul II frequently reiterated for the whole Church the extraordinary value of the rosary.

Above all, the Church wants us to know that "the Eucharistic Sacrifice of Christ is the source and summit of the whole Christian life."

III

Gaudium et Spes:
Joy and Hope
in the Modern World

The Second Vatican Council gave us many great gifts. One
of these was the Pastoral Constitution on the Church in the
Modern World. This document was called *Gaudium et Spes,*
after the first words of the Latin text. It was promulgated
on December 7, 1965, the last day of the Council. So much
of the flavor of this document is already present in the first
sentence which reads: "The joys and the hopes, the griefs
and the anxieties of the people of this age, especially those
who are poor or in any way afflicted, are also the joys and
hopes, the griefs and anxieties of the followers of Christ."

　　　This is a very lofty vision expressing the outreach of
the Church to the world. It shows to what degree the Council
envisioned solidarity with all people. In this document
the Church was proposing to speak to the world and to all
humanity. She was proposing to tell the world how she
conceives her own presence and activity in the midst of the
world. The document had actually been proposed at the
end of the first session of the Council, three years before.
This was done by Cardinal Suenens of Belgium. The idea
was backed at that time also by Cardinal Giovanni Battista
Montini of Milan, later to become Pope Paul VI.

What is immediately apparent in the document is the continuity of its teaching. Much of its social content echoes the teaching of Leo XIII, Pius XI, Pius XII, and John XXIII, especially the famous encyclicals *Mater et Magistra* and *Pacem in Terris*. It is worth noting right away that the teaching of *Gaudium et Spes* was vigorously proclaimed throughout the world by Pope John Paul II during all the years of his pontificate. The document, which is called a *pastoral constitution,* proposes to speak to all people in order to shed light on *the mystery of man*. It does this in an effort to help find solutions to the outstanding problems of our time.

The document has two main divisions. Part I is "The Church and Man's Calling"; Part II is "Some More Urgent Questions."

Part I has four chapters which we could summarize as follows: 1) the dignity of the human person, 2) the community of mankind, 3) human activity throughout the world, and 4) the mission of the Church in the modern world.

Part II, which treats the urgent questions facing the world, has five chapters. These are 1) fostering the dignity of marriage and the family, 2) the proper promotion of the development of culture, 3) socioeconomic life, 4) the life of the political community, and 5) the promotion of peace and the community of peoples.

Dignity of the Human Person: Conscience and Freedom

In Part I, chapter one immediately faces the important question of *the dignity of the human person*. This will be basic to everything else in the document. This will be presumed in everything else in the document. And the Council sees this

dignity of the human person as being linked to the fact that
the human person is created by God, redeemed by Christ,
and called to communion with God for all eternity.
Incidentally, this will be one of the favorite themes of John
Paul II during all the years of his pontificate. He will
constantly be inspired by this conciliar vision. In season and
out of season, he will proclaim the dignity of the human
person. Linked to the dignity of the human person are the
questions of *conscience* and *human freedom.* The Council
describes *conscience,* saying: "In the depths of his conscience,
man detects a law which he does not impose upon himself,
but which he is bound to obey. Always summoning him to
love good and avoid evil, the voice of conscience can when
necessary speak to his heart more specifically: Do this.
Shun that. For man has in his heart a law written by God.
To obey it is the very dignity of man. According to it he
will be judged" (no. 16).

Intimately linked to the theme of conscience is that
of *freedom.* The Council insists that the dignity of the
human being demands that he act according to a knowing
and free choice. In effect, God wanted the human being to
be able to say *no* precisely so that his *yes* would be authentic
and meritorious.

Two other themes that vex the human spirit are
considered in the pastoral constitution: the question
of *death* with its perennial mystery and the issue of *atheism.*
The Council asserts that atheism must be counted among
the more serious problems of this age and is deserving of
closer examination. A key statement is found in no. 22 as
the Council shows the relationship of its Christology to the
human being with this bold assertion: "The truth is that
only in the mystery of the Incarnate Word does the mystery
of man take on life." It gives a reason for this statement,

adding: "By his Incarnation the Son of God has united himself in some fashion with every man.

The Gospel as Inspiration for Mankind

The vision of human dignity presented in chapter one is enlarged in chapter two to take into account the *community of mankind.* Here the Council's insights are deep and ever relevant. It says: "One of the salient features of the modern world is the growing interdependence of people on each other, a development very largely promoted by modern technological advancements" (no. 23). It goes on to explain, however, that authentic dialogue among people does not reach its perfection on the level of technical progress but on the deeper level of *interpersonal relationships.* Here the Council is emphasizing the communitarian nature of the vocation of human beings as one family. It is speaking of the interdependence of individuals and society, with the goal of all social institutions remaining *the human person.* Human interdependence grows more tightly and the notion of the common good takes on an increasingly universal complexion involving rights and duties with respect to the whole human race. This interdependence and common good open up to us the whole notion of universal *solidarity.*

Later on in *Gaudium et Spes* we will find a remarkable text about the truth of our identity as human beings. It states: "We are witnesses of the birth of a new humanism, one in which man is defined first of all by his responsibility to his brothers and sisters and toward history" (no. 55). I submit that the birth of a new humanism is very much connected, whenever it occurs, with the activities of Catholic education, and that the "new humanism" of Vatican II—the humanism of solidarity, indeed of man being defined in

relationship to others, must be an evangelical guiding light
for the orientation of all Catholic education. What great
dignity, what great responsibility, what a great mission is
entrusted to the human person! And what service Catholic
education can fulfill in being a herald of this "new humanism"!

Years later, in 1987, Pope John Paul II amply developed the theme of solidarity and the act proper to it, which
is *collaboration,* in his encyclical letter *Sollicitudo Rei Socialis.*
Included in this second chapter is also a splendid treatment
of *reverence for the human person.* This emphasis by the
Council has subsequently been magnificently developed by
John Paul II in his encyclical the Gospel of Life and in
many other documents. Here the Council gives us a summary of what is opposed to this human dignity. It says:
"Whatever is opposed to life itself, such as any type of mur-
der, genocide, abortion, euthanasia or willful self-destruction;
whatever violates the integrity of the human person, such as
mutilation, torments inflicted on body or mind, attempts to
coerce the will itself; whatever insults human dignity such
as subhuman living conditions, arbitrary imprisonment,
deportation, slavery, prostitution, the selling of women and
children; as well as disgraceful working conditions where
people are treated as mere tools for profit rather than as
free and responsible persons. All of this and the like are
infamies indeed. They poison human society, but they do
more harm to those who practice them than those who
suffer from the injury. Moreover, they are a supreme
dishonor to the Creator" (no. 27).

It was also to be expected that in speaking about
human dignity and the essential equality of peoples that the
Council would reject "every type of discrimination, whether
social or cultural, whether based on sex, race, color, social
condition, language, or religion" (no. 29).

The Council complained that fundamental personal rights are not yet universally honored as in "the case of a woman who is denied the right and freedom to choose a husband, to embrace a state of life or to acquire an education or cultural benefits equal to those recognized for men" (ibid.).

In chapter three, no. 33, the Council spoke about the Church's *religious and moral principles* that derive from the heritage of God's word, but which do not always have at hand the solution to particular problems. The Council admits clearly that it does not offer ready-made solutions to the many problems of the world, but rather sees the Gospel as the guide and the source of the principles that will respond to the issues of the modern world. At the beginning of the document the Council had already said that the Church always has had the duty of scrutinizing the signs of the times and interpreting them in the light of the Gospel. And thus she is able to respond to the perennial questions that are presented to her without at the same time having simplistic solutions to every problem. Gospel principles in the life of the Church will be crystal clear, but their application will involve prayer and openness to the Spirit of Truth.

Making the Human Family More Human

Chapter four treats *the mission of the Church* in the modern world. Here the Council expresses the conviction that the Church believes that she can contribute greatly toward making the human family and its history more human. The Church holds in high esteem and values the contribution of other Christian churches and ecclesial communities and of all human society. A special part of the Church's mission is to proclaim human rights.

In the aftermath of the Council, Pope Paul VI and John Paul II would lead the world in the implementation of this proclamation. In 1967, just shortly after the close of Vatican II, Paul VI would issue his great encyclical "The Development of Peoples." Two years later, in Africa, and on many other occasions he would vigorously supplement this by his personal teaching. John Paul II would fall heir both to the Council and to Paul VI. The incarnational spirituality of *Gaudium et Spes* was evident as it proclaimed that the split between the faith that many people profess and their daily lives deserves to be counted among "the more serious errors of our age" (no. 43). It further stated that there can be no false opposition between professional and social activities on the one hand and religious life on the other. In perfect harmony with the Gospel it further went on to assert: "The Christian who neglects his temporal duties neglects his duties toward his neighbor and even God, and jeopardizes his eternal salvation" (no. 43).

Part II of *Gaudium et Spes* presents to the consideration of the world five crucial issues of special urgency and particular relevance. These issues are *the dignity of marriage and the family, the proper promotion of development of culture, socioeconomic life, the life of the political community,* and, finally, fostering peace and the international community.

The Council's treatment of marriage in the family begins out with a recognition of the great challenges that face the family today. In this context the Council proclaims *the sanctity* of marriage and the family and the entire Catholic doctrine of Christian married love and Christian married life.

The Council zeros in on the *centrality of conjugal love* and the concept of *a covenant relationship* between two people in which marriage and conjugal love are by their nature ordained toward the begetting and the educating of children. The Council asserts that the intimate partnership of married

life and love has been established by the Creator and made
subject to His laws. It is rooted in the conjugal covenant of
irrevocable personal consent. The Council speaks of children
as *the supreme gift of marriage.* Anticipating the encyclical
Humanae Vitae the Council asserts that "when there is a
question of harmonizing conjugal love the responsible transmission of life, the moral aspect of any procedure does not
depend solely on sincere intentions or an evaluation of
motives" (no. 51). This aim of the Council to inculcate the
dignity of marriage in the family is certainly today a tre-
mendous support for married couples as they endeavor to
fulfill their great mission of human and Christian love in
the Church and in the world.

Catholic Culture

The second issue to which the Council devoted its attention
is *culture.* The Council stated that the human being can
only come to an authentic and full expression of his humanity
through culture. The Council attempted to give an adequate description of culture saying that it indicates all those
aspects by which a human being refines and unfolds his or
her manifold spiritual and bodily quality. It is a feature of
culture that throughout history man expresses, communi-
cates, and preserves in his works great spiritual experiences
and desires. In this sense we can speak so fittingly of *Catholic
culture.* People are conscious, the Council says, that they
themselves can be the artisans and authors of the culture
of their community. This presumes a sense of responsibility
and solidarity. In this context the Council says that we
are witnesses of the birth of *a new humanism,* one in which
*the human being is defined especially by his responsibility
toward his brothers and sisters and toward history.* In the

humanization of the world, how important it is that each person realize his or her responsibility to others.

In chapter three of part II, the Council speaks about *socioeconomic life*, placing all economic development at the service of man, the human being, the human person. Two years later in the Encyclical on the Development of Peoples already mentioned, Pope Paul VI will develop this theme beautifully.

Gaudium et Spes then speaks about *human labor*— how it is superior to all the other elements of economic life, and how man himself is a partner in the work of bringing God's creation to perfection. In 1981 John Paul II developed in his Encyclical *Laborem Exercens* the whole theology of work. In this encyclical Pope John Paul II will present human work as a *key to the whole social question of our day*. While seeing private ownership and property as an expression of human freedom, the Council also speaks of the profound plan of God in which there is a common destination for created things and in which all human beings are called to recognize interdependence and exercise solidarity. In chapter three the Council has initiated us into a great reflection on *solidarity and globalization*.

In chapter four, *Gaudium et Spes* makes it clear that the political community exists for the common good. This political community and public authority are based on human nature and belong to an order of things divinely foreordained. For this reason those who serve in politics contribute greatly to the building up of society. The political community and the Church are mutually independent and self-governing but they both serve the personal and social vocation of the same human beings in accordance with the truth of humanity. Catholic politicians are expected to bring to their service of the community those principles based on the natural law, inscribed in the human heart and which are also proclaimed by the Church.

In recent times this political participation of Catholics according to their own upright consciences has been amply reinforced and clarified by the Congregation for the Doctrine of the Faith. It would exclude any reasoning such as: "Personally I am opposed to the destruction of human life, but if there is a political consensus, then so be it."

Peace for All Humanity

Gaudium et Spes concludes by turning the attention of the world to the subject of *peace:* the fostering of peace and the promotion of a community of nations. It makes clear that it is speaking about a peace that is based on justice and love. It makes clear that by peace it does not mean only the absence of war, but rather the work of justice.

The Council draws greatly in this regard on the encyclical of Pope John XXIII, *Pacem in Terris.* Even as the Fathers of the Second Vatican Council were preparing to issue this appeal, Pope Paul VI was visiting the United Nations on October 4, 1965, pleading for the avoidance of war and at the same time expressing hope that nations would come together in a spirit of harmony to understand the basic need for harmony in the world. The position of the Holy See has constantly been that the United Nations, notwithstanding its weaknesses and limitation, is a structure that the world cannot prescind from and that can be helped to fulfill a role of peace for all humanity.

Gaudium et Spes also expressed its conviction that there should be an agency of the universal Church set up for the worldwide promotion of justice and for charity for the poor. After the Ecumenical Council, the Pontifical

Council for Justice and Peace and the Pontifical Council *Cor Unum* were both established to serve the needs recognized by Vatican II.

The Pastoral Constitution on the Church came to life on the very last day of the Council. It was a beautiful sign of Christian hope for the world, with a beautiful ecumenical dimension. It was a clear sign of the Church's willingness for dialogue within the Church, with those not in full communion with her, for those who believe in God and for those also who do not as yet acknowledge God, and even with those who oppress the Church. It was a great sign of the *Church's desire to serve,* and in this it represented the highest ideal of the Church that imitates Christ, who says: "I have come not to be served, but to serve."

IV

The Instruments
of Social Communication:
Communicating God's Love

The Second Vatican Council had every reason to treat
the subject of *social communications*. The Church herself
is the Church of the Eternal Word, who is the expression
of the Father and His communication to the world. All
true communication shares in God's communication
of His Word. My own episcopal motto, *Verbum caro factum
est*, draws attention to the fact that the Word became flesh.
God communicated supremely to the world when His
Word became flesh in the womb of the Virgin Mary.

So much of the activity of the Church is communication. Our Lord Jesus Christ has commanded His Apostles
to communicate the Gospel, indeed to communicate Him
through the Gospel. The mission of the Church is to evangelize in season and out of season. This means communicating the good news of God's love and His gift of salvation
and mercy in Jesus Christ.

All the catechetical activity of the Church is one
aspect of evangelization, one systematic aspect of communicating the Gospel.

Marvelous Inventions

Since Vatican II, communications in the world are radically changed and yet the ideals of Vatican II remain the same.

The Decree called *Inter Mirifica* of Vatican II was the first Decree promulgated, together with the first Constitution, which was that of the Sacred Liturgy. The two documents were signed at the end of the second session of Vatican II, on December 4, 1963. I had the privilege of being present.

What was the Decree about? And why was the Council treating this matter?

The Council answers these questions. It spoke about the instruments of communication as being *marvelous inventions* through which the Church can reach great multitudes, indeed all of society itself. Vatican II saw these marvelous inventions in relationship to the good of humanity and to building up the Kingdom of God.

The Demands of Truth and Justice

The Council made a special point of hoping that its principles would be not only for the spiritual good of the faithful but for the progress of all humanity.

The document has two chapters. Chapter one enunciates *the norms for the right use of the means of social communication.*

The Church considers it her duty to use these means to preach the Gospel, and also to speak about their correct use.

To use these instruments properly, it is necessary for the users to know the norms of morality that apply to them: to know the demands of truth and justice.

The Council sustained *the right of people to information.* The content must be true, and justice and charity are to be observed in its transmission.

Vatican II spoke about the treatment of moral evil, public opinion, and the duties of readers, viewers, and listeners.

The Council endeavored to guide young people and parents, authors, and civil authorities.

Chapter two presents the instruments of social communication and *the Catholic apostolate.*

Vatican II encouraged the Bishops and the faithful to use the means of social communication effectively. What is at stake is *bearing witness to Christ.*

The Council recognized the importance in the Holy See of having an Office for social communications. This is now called the Pontifical Council for Social Communications.

For over twenty years this office has been headed by an American, Archbishop John Foley of Philadelphia, who has been an encouragement to communicators throughout the world. This Pontifical Council has unceasingly promoted the Church's use of the media in the spirit of Vatican II.

The Council appealed to those who control the media to use them only for the good of humanity.

Humanity More Dependent on the Media

In our own experience each one of us can verify the concluding words of the Decree, which says that "the fate of humanity grows daily more dependent on the right use of these media."

In his many journeys around the world Pope John Paul II had numerous meetings with people of the media. He has had numerous opportunities to express once again

the teaching of the Church in regard to the proper use of
the media, but he also had numerous opportunities *to thank
the media for the great mission they have of presenting truth to
the world.* Personally, he was deeply indebted to the world
media for being able through them to reach millions and
millions of people upon the face of the earth. Each one
of his apostolic journeys around the world, each one of his
pastoral visits depended for its full success on the contribution of the media. It is the media that brought John Paul II,
the Catholic Church and her teaching into millions of
homes throughout the world. It is the media that brought
the Holy Father and his message into contact with millions
of people over the face of the globe, both during his lifetime
and, in an unforgettable and magnificent way, at the time
of his funeral and the election of his successor. The Church
continues to bless God for the many opportunities that
are given through these marvelous instruments of social
communication *to proclaim the Gospel.*

V

The Eastern Churches:
East and West,
Together in the Church

The decree on the Eastern Churches is a very short decree
of the Second Vatican Council. But it shows *the incredible
beauty of the Catholic Church*. Pope John Paul II constantly
emphasized the need for the Church to breathe with two
lungs: with the lung of *the East* and the lung of *the West*.
The reason for this is the nature of the Church, her teaching, her tradition. The Decree on the Eastern Churches
is the solemn proclamation of the nature of the one Church
of Christ, made up of Eastern, or Oriental, Churches and
the Latin Church of the West.

   The document begins citing a decree of Pope Leo
XIII in 1894. It was called *Orientalium Dignitas,* proclaiming
the dignity of the Eastern Churches and all those who
make them up. The message is exhilarating and important
in its consequences. Leo XIII and Vatican II sought to safeguard the Eastern traditions for the whole Church. The
purpose of the Council in adopting this decree was to support the Eastern Churches so that they would take on, in
the words of the Council, a "new apostolic vigor" (no. 1).

Unity and Equal Dignity

For this reason the Council laid down some important principles. There is a variety of different rites or usages in the Church, and this variety does anything but harm the unity. Indeed, it manifests unity. At the same time all of the particular Churches, whether of the East or of the West, are entrusted to the Successor of Peter, as the supreme pastor and Vicar of Christ for all the Churches. Their dignity and authenticity consists in their being in communion with *the Roman Pontiff* and, through him, in communion with *the whole Church of Christ*.

It was clearly pointed out that all of the particular Churches are of equal dignity. The preservation and growth of the individual Churches are to be promoted. In addition, the Council went on record as saying that *parishes and hierarchies* should be established where the spiritual good of the faithful demands it.

How solicitous the Church has been in providing new Eastern rite dioceses or eparchies in the United States. Most of us are probably not familiar with the impressive list of the Eastern Catholic eparchies, archeparchies, and exarchates. The list includes the following:

- Armenian Catholic Exarchate of the United States and Canada (New York City)
- Byzantine Metropolitan Archeparchy of Pittsburgh
- Byzantine Eparchy of Parma (Ohio)
- Byzantine Eparchy of Passaic (West Paterson, New Jersey)
- Byzantine Eparchy of Van Nuys (Phoenix, Arizona)
- Chaldean Eparchy of St. Thomas the Apostle (Southfield, Michigan)

- Chaldean Eparchy of St. Peter the Apostle (San Diego, California)
- Maronite Eparchy of Our Lady of Lebanon of St. Louis
- Maronite Eparchy of St. Maron in Brooklyn
- Melkite Eparchy of Newton (Brookline, Massachusetts)
- Our Lady of Deliverance Syriac Catholic Diocese in the United States and Canada (Union City, New Jersey)
- Romanian Eparchy of St. George in Canton, Ohio
- St. Thomas Syro-Malabar Eparchy of Chicago
- Ukrainian Metropolitan Archeparchy of Philadelphia
- Ukrainian Eparchy of St. Josaphat in Parma, Ohio
- Ukrainian Eparchy of St. Nicholas in Chicago
- Ukrainian Eparchy of Stamford, Connecticut

Eastern Catholics: Enriching Collaboration and Spiritual Legacy

How enriching all these Eastern rite Churches are for the Catholics who belong to them, for the Church throughout the United States and also for the universal Church!

Another principle embraced by the Council is that there should be *collaboration* among Ordinaries and where possible, unity of action. The Eastern Rite Bishops of the United States are members of the United States Catholic Conference of Bishops. They participate in the work of the Conference as do the Latin Bishops; they share the solicitude of all the Bishops for the good of the Church throughout the United States. The one area in which they are not present in the discussions of the body of Bishops in the United States is the liturgical field, because all of these dioceses have their own liturgies that are recognized by the Holy See.

As the former Archbishop of St. Louis, I am very proud of *the Maronite community in St. Louis.* I am proud of the example of unity that exists between the Latin Church and the Maronite Church and the splendid collaboration that has taken place over the years. As Archbishop of Philadelphia I am very proud of the excellent relations existing with the Ukrainian Church.

The Second Vatican Council desires that the clergy and the laity alike be instructed about their respective rites and the norms of those rites. So interested is Vatican II in the preservation of the rites that it prescribes that whoever enters the Catholic Church should, in general, enter his or her respective rite in the Catholic Church. This is a norm that concerns those Orthodox faithful who are coming into full communion with the Catholic Church.

The Council expresses the Church's debt to *the* Eastern Churches. Vatican II honors the ecclesiastical and *spiritual heritage of these Eastern Churches* and considers it the heritage of the universal Church (cf. no. 5).

How magnificent for the universal Church is *the legacy of the great Fathers of the Church,* like Saint Basil the Great, Saint Gregory Nazianzen, Saint Gregory of Nyssa, Saint John Chrysostom, Saint Athanasius, and others.

According to the Council, there should be a preservation of liturgical rites and practices. And this should remain unaltered except for *the appropriate organic development* of these rites and practices.

The institution of *the patriarchate* is recognized by the Council as dating back to the earliest of times (no. 7). Some of the partriarchates are of later origin, but all of them are equal in patriarchal dignity, while there is still an order of precedence (no. 8).

There are six Eastern Patriarchs in the Catholic Church: The *Coptic* Patriarch of Alexandria; the Melkite Patriarch of Antioch, who has also the title of Alexandria and Jerusalem; the *Syrian* and the *Maronite* Patriarchs, who have the title of Antioch; and the *Armenian* and the *Chaldean* Patriarchs. In keeping with the most ancient tradition of the Church, the Patriarchs of the Eastern Churches are to be accorded exceptional respect since each one presides over his patriarchate as father and head. Each patriarch is in communion with the Bishop of Rome, the Successor of Peter, the Head of the College of Bishops, and the Pastor of the universal Church.

In 2001, in St. Louis we had for the first time the visit of Patriarch Sfeir of the Maronite Church. It was a great honor for us to receive him. The Patriarch came to St. Louis to visit his own Maronite faithful. On that occasion, he ordained to the episcopate the first Maronite Bishop born in the United States: Bishop Robert Shaheen of the Eparchy of Our Lady of Lebanon. The Maronite Church accepted the hospitality of our Cathedral and the Patriarch ordained Bishop Shaheen in the Cathedral Basilica of Saint Louis, which was larger than their own Cathedral of Saint Raymond.

I also experienced the honor of being received by Patriarch Sfeir in Lebanon where he gave me the opportunity to address the meeting of all the Maronite Bishops. These exchanges are exchanges that are made within *the full communion of the Catholic Church*. We are all united in the one holy Catholic faith. We have different traditions in the East and in the West, different legacies but all of these are fully Catholic.

What an enrichment it is for St. Louis to have constant contact with *the Eparchy of Our Lady of Lebanon.* As the Latin Archbishop I was always received with warmth and respect by the entire Maronite community. Patriarch Sfeir was to return to St. Louis for a second Pastoral visit but it had to be postponed because of the world situation.

Although there are no other Eastern Bishops in St. Louis, there are other Eastern Catholics including the Byzantine Catholics and the Ukrainian Catholics. In the past, I was able to show solidarity with both of these Churches by being present in Ukraine for the visit of Pope John Paul II with the Major Archbishop, Cardinal Husar. I was also able to assist at the Enthronement of Archbishop Basil Schott as the Byzantine Metropolitan Archbishop of Pittsburgh.

The Decree on the Eastern Catholic Churches also gave practical norms concerning *sacramental discipline.* The Council expressed the ardent desire that the permanent diaconate be restored in those Eastern Churches where it had fallen into disuse. The theme of maximum importance treated by the Decree on the Eastern Catholic Churches is the question of the relations of Eastern Catholics with their brethren of separated Churches. The Council saw a special role for the Eastern Catholic Churches in promoting the unity of all Christians, especially the Orthodox. The means suggested are prayer, the example of Christian living, religious fidelity to ancient Eastern traditions, greater mutual knowledge, and collaboration.

Eastern Christians: Still Separated but Nourished by the Same Faith and Sacraments

Because of the Church's great respect not only for the Eastern Catholic Churches but also for the Eastern Christians who are separated in good faith from the Catholic Church, the Council has legislated that if these Christians "ask of their own accord and have the right dispositions they may be granted the Sacraments of Penance, the Eucharist and the Anointing of the Sick. Furthermore, Catholics may ask for these same sacraments from those non-Catholic ministers whose Churches possess valid sacraments, as often as necessity or a genuine spiritual benefit recommends such a course of action and when access to a Catholic priest is physically or morally impossible" (no. 27).

This norm on the part of the Catholic Church is *a respectful offer made to the Eastern Orthodox Churches on behalf of their faithful.* It is not meant to take the faithful away from the Orthodox Churches, but merely to make available spiritual ministry. The norms that apply to Catholics approaching Eastern Orthodox Churches presume that access to a Catholic priest is physically or morally impossible.

In its conclusion, Vatican II looks forward with hope to *the eventual union of all the Eastern Churches in the one Church of Jesus Christ.* This union would create a new situation when the present norms would no longer apply. The document concludes by stating: "This sacred Council feels great joy in the fruitful and zealous collaboration between the Eastern and the Western Catholic Churches, and at the same time declares that all these directives of law are laid down in view of the present situation until such time as the Catholic Church and the separated Eastern Churches come together into complete unity.

"Meanwhile however all Christians, Eastern as well as Western, are earnestly asked to pray to God fervently and insistently, indeed daily, that with the aid of the Most Holy Mother of God all may become one" (no. 30).

Like Pope John XXIII and Pope Paul VI, Pope John Paul II constantly promoted Christian unity. In particular, he drew attention to *all the many Christian martyrs* whose common witness to Christ is a strong reason to promote Christian unity.

The Decree on the Eastern Catholic Churches has entered into the life of the Church in the last four decades. Pope John Paul II was *a special champion of the Christian East,* passionately working and praying and traveling to promote unity between East and West, to highlight the profound contribution of the Christian East to the universal Church. In doing so, he was inspired by the great example of the Second Vatican Council. Over and over again he proclaimed this teaching in word and action, giving new impetus to the important emphasis of the Church's "two lungs." As recently as the feast of Corpus Christi 2005, Pope Benedict XVI has renewed the commitment of the Church and of his predecessors to work for the reunion of all Christians. He did this in the Italian city of Ban, where East meets West.

In 1995 Pope John Paul II wrote an Apostolic Letter entitled *Orientale Lumen,* "Light of the East," which he identifies as "Jesus Christ our Lord, whom all Christians invoke as the Redeemer of man and the hope of the world" (no. 1).

The Holy Father explained that this Light of the East was what inspired Pope Leo XIII in 1894 to write his Apostolic Letter *Orientalium Dignitas,* which in turn was an important source of Vatican II's document on the Eastern Catholic Churches.

Be Familiar with the Tradition

Pope John Paul II reformulated in elegant words the great esteem of the universal Church for the East. He said: "Since, in fact, we believe that the venerable and ancient tradition of the Eastern Churches is an integral part of the heritage of Christ's Church, the first need for Catholics is *to be familiar with that tradition,* so as to be nourished by it and to encourage the process of unity in the best way possible for each.

"Our Eastern Catholic brothers and sisters are very conscious of being the living bearers of this tradition together with our Orthodox brothers and sisters. The members of the Catholic Church of the Latin tradition must also be fully acquainted with this treasure and thus feel with the Pope a passionate longing that the full manifestation of the Church's catholicity be restored to the Church and to the world, expressed not by a single tradition and still less by one community in opposition to the other; and that we too may be granted a full taste of the divinely revealed and undivided heritage of the universal Church which is preserved and grows in the life of the Churches of the East as in those of the West" (no. 1).

The Pope clearly showed the close link between Eastern Christianity and the cause of Christian unity.

The Apostolic Letter *Orientale Lumen,* "Light of the East," is a magnificent commentary and amplification of the Church's teaching of Vatican II. In supporting this teaching the Pope says: "The Christian tradition of the East implies a way of accepting, understanding and living faith in the Lord Jesus. In this sense it is extremely close to the Christian tradition of the West, which is born and nourished by the same faith. Yet, it is legitimately and admirably distinguished from the latter. Since Eastern Christians have their own way of perceiving and understanding, and thus an original way of living their relationship with the Savior" (no. 10).

Pope John Paul II then launched into a splendid analysis of *the Trinitarian dimension of the Eastern liturgies*. In doing so, he engendered in the universal Church a sense of solidarity and pride in the contribution of Eastern theology and piety, culture, and art.

Love, Admiration, and Shared Conversion

As the Pope yearned and reached out to promote greater unity with the East, he recalled the cause of historical estrangement with part of the East. He identified it as a lack of perception of each other's diversity as being not a common treasure, but incompatibility. He recalled with joy the abrogation by Pope Paul VI and the Ecumenical Patriarch of Constantinople Anthenagoras I of the reciprocal excommunications of the year 1054 between East and West.

If I may interject a parenthesis. For the last eight and a half years of the life of Pope Paul VI, I had the great honor of being the English language translator for the Holy Father in his private audiences. I remember on one occasion in a private audience how the question of Patriarch Athenagoras came up. The Pope's face became radiant. He beamed. He spoke in terms of immense love and admiration for this great man from the East precisely because Christian unity and the harmony of East and West were so dear to the heart of Athenagoras as they were to the heart of Pope Paul VI and after him, so dear to the heart of John Paul II, and now to Pope Benedict XVI.

Both Vatican II and Pope John Paul II have shown a deep particular love for *the Eastern Churches that are in full communion with Rome.* These Churches merit deep respect and understanding. In addition to all the challenges of being a holy part of the Church, these Eastern Catholic Churches, in the words of John Paul II, "carry a tragic wound for they are still kept from full communion with the Eastern Orthodox Churches, despite sharing in the heritage of their fathers. *A constant shared conversion is indispensable* for them to advance resolutely and energetically toward mutual understanding. And conversion is also required of the Latin Church, that she may respect and fully appreciate the dignity of Eastern Christians, and accept gratefully the spiritual treasures of which the Eastern Catholic Churches are the bearers, to the benefit of the entire Catholic communion" (no. 21).

One very practical conclusion of the Council's teaching on the Eastern Catholic Churches is expressed in Pope John Paul II's comment: "I believe that one important way to grow in mutual understanding and unity consists precisely in improving our knowledge of one another" (no. 24).

One of the various ways that Pope John Paul II proposed to do this was through knowledge of the liturgy of the Eastern Churches. To do this we are helped by all the Eastern rites in the United States. It is a wonderful contribution to unity and a great gift to the universal Church. Together with Vatican II, we renew our solidarity—Catholics of the Eastern and Western traditions—in the unity of a single Church that is one, holy, Catholic, and apostolic.

VI

Ecumenism: Toward the Unity of All Christ's Followers

The Decree on Ecumenism of the Second Vatican Council begins out by saying that *promoting the restoration of unity among all Christians* is one of the chief concerns of the Second Vatican Council. To understand why the Church gives this great priority to this particular work, it is necessary to understand the great passionate love of Christ Himself, which we find revealed in the seventeenth chapter of Saint John's Gospel. There we see that Christ prays for the unity of all His followers. He prays "that they may be one" and the reason He prays "that they may be one" is "that the world may believe."

If Jesus Himself prays to His Father for this intention—the unity of all His followers—then it is some-thing that is uppermost in His Sacred Heart. It is a cause that He has bequeathed to the Church. And so the Second Vatican Council, in its deliberate desire to be faithful to Christ, commits itself to *the cause of ecumenism*. That cause of ecumenism is promoting the restoration of unity among all Christians.

The Decree on Ecumenism is divided into three chapters: 1) the Catholic principles of ecumenism, 2) the exercise of ecumenism, and 3) Churches and ecclesial communities that are separated from the Catholic Church.

Longing for Unity

In the introduction to the Decree on Ecumenism, the
Council right away speaks about a grace that God has been
bestowing more generously in recent years on divided
Christians—Christians that are divided among themselves.
The Council calls this remorse over their divisions and
a longing for unity.

The Council recognizes that there is today a movement in the world. It is fostered by the grace of the Holy
Spirit, and it is directed to the restoration of unity among
all Christians. There are many individuals who are moved
by this remorse and motivated by this longing for unity.
There are many groups who likewise pursue these ends.
And so, at this point, the Ecumenical Council Vatican II
sets before Catholics the principles of ecumenism that they
are to follow. At the same time it explains how they are to
apply these principles.

In the first chapter of the Decree, the Council points
out that the prayer that Christ made to His Father took
place before He sacrificed Himself on the Cross. His prayer
was "that they may all be one, as you, Father, are in me and
I in you, that they also may be in us, that the world may
believe that you sent me" (John 17:21). The day after Jesus
spoke these words, He offered His life in sacrifice on
Calvary. And the high priest Caiaphas, Saint John tells us,
had prophesied that Jesus was going to die for the nation
and not only for the nation, but also to gather into one the
dispersed children of God (cf. John 11:52). As a matter of
fact, the death of Jesus, which we renew in the Eucharistic
sacrifice, we offer constantly to fulfill the intentions of
Christ's prayer "that all may be one" and that the dispersed
children of God may be gathered into one.

Christ established His Church as one. And even as we pray for the unity of all Christians, even as we pray that all the dispersed children of God may be gathered into one, we are still mindful that the unity that Christ gave to His Church dwells indestructibly in the Catholic Church. And this unity finds its highest exemplar and source in the mystery of the Most Blessed Trinity, in the communion of the Father, the Son, and the Holy Spirit (cf. no. 2). But Christ's intention is that all His followers might be united in one mind and one heart, in one faith, one Lord, one Baptism, one Church.

Vatican II goes back to the writings of the Apostles and points out how there were rifts in the Church almost from the beginning, and in subsequent centuries more widespread disagreements occurred, which in turn became separation from the full communion of the Catholic Church. Vatican II acknowledges that the sin of separation is not to be imputed to those who inherit the sin. It admits that at times people on both sides share blame for the separation. In addition, many of the elements of separated communities are gifts that are found in the Catholic Church. The Council tells us that these gifts can exist outside the visible boundaries of the Church. These include the written word of God, the life of grace, the theological virtues—faith, hope, and charity—the interior gifts of the Holy Spirit, and various visible elements, beginning with Baptism.

Vatican II asserts that all of these elements come from Christ and they lead back to Christ, and they belong by right to the Church of Christ. Vatican II acknowledges that the separated Churches and ecclesial communities have still been used by the Holy Spirit as means of salvation and that they derive their efficacy from the *very fullness of grace and truth that was entrusted to the Catholic Church.*

Love, Esteem, and Affection

The Council expresses immense love, esteem and affection for all individual separated Christians and for the various Churches and ecclesial communities to which they belong. And yet, with the honesty of profound interior conviction, Vatican II asserts that it is through Christ's Catholic Church alone, which is the all-embracing means of salvation, that the fullness of the means of salvation can be obtained. It is neither arrogance nor triumphalism, but the profound conviction of faith that Christ Himself established one Church which He committed to Peter and the other Apostles.

Besides admitting the action of the Holy Spirit in separated Christians and in their communities, the Church has also recognized in them extraordinary fruits of holiness. And, in a very special way, the pontificate of John Paul II drew attention to *the numerous martyrs for Christ* that are another witness to the need for the restoration of the unity of all Christians in the one Body of Christ, drawing attention to the fact that in many parts of the world the Holy Spirit is active in inspiring prayer and action to attain the full unity that Christ desires. Speaking to Catholics, Vatican II urges them to recognize "the signs of the times" and to participate in ecumenism.

The Decree on Ecumenism describes *the ecumenical movement* as embracing *all of the activities and enterprises that foster unity among Christians.* Here we come to a very important and practical dimension of ecumenism. These activities and enterprises include eliminating words, judgments, and actions that do not represent the condition of our separated brothers and sisters with truth and fairness. The Decree urges dialogue between competent experts in different churches and ecclesial communities. It proposes cooperation in projects that the Christian conscience demands for the common good.

The Council speaks about common prayer and the examination of one's own faithfulness to Christ's will for the Church. At this point the Council recommends that, wherever necessary, we undertake with vigor *the task of renewal and reform,* which begins with ourselves personally. The Council sees the result of all of this as being little by little the elimination of obstacles to perfect ecclesial communion, with Christians finally being gathered in a common celebration of the Eucharist, into the unity of the one and only Church that Christ established.

Vatican II speaks about ecumenical work involving prayers for the separated Christian brothers and sisters and the need to keep them informed about the Church, and in making first approaches to them. But, at the same time, it draws the attention of Catholics that they are charged especially to make an honest and careful appraisal of whatever needs to be renewed and brought about in the Catholic household itself, in order that Catholic life may bear witness more faithfully and more luminously to the teachings of Christ and His Apostles.

Although the Catholic Church has been endowed with all divinely revealed truth, with all the means of grace, this does not mean that her members live by them with all the fervor they should. By reason of human failures, the radiance of Christ's face shines less brightly for our separated brethren and the growth of God's kingdom is affected. All Catholics are called to play their part, so that the Church may daily be purified and renewed until the time when Christ will present her to His Father in all her glory. It is important for Catholics to recognize the riches of Christ and virtuous works in the lives of our separated brethren.

Renewal in Fidelity to Our Calling

The second chapter of the Decree on Ecumenism is dedicated to *the practice of ecumenism*. The depth and beauty of this chapter is outstanding. This chapter begins by speaking of the concern for the restoration of Christian unity and how this concern itself leads toward that full and perfect unity which God Himself desires. Here Vatican II explains what it means by renewal, saying that "every renewal of the Church essentially consists in an increase in fidelity to her own calling." It states that Christ summons the Church, as she goes her pilgrim way, to that continual reformation of which she is always in need to the extent that she is a human institution here on earth. Whatever is defective in the conduct of the faithful, in Church discipline or even in the formulation of doctrine, must be appropriately rectified. The Council distinguishes clearly in this last element between *the formulation of doctrine* and *the very deposit of faith.*

The Council shows that the renewal of the Church has ecumenical import. Biblical and liturgical movements, the preaching of the word of God, catechetics, the apostolate of the laity, new forms of religious life, and the spirituality of married life in the Church's social teaching and activity are all looked upon as pledges and signs of ecumenical progress in the future.

Numbers seven and eight of chapter two contain ecumenical insights of extraordinary depth that show *the profound spirituality of the Second Vatican Council.* We are told that there can be no true ecumenism without *a change of heart,* without *conversion* in other words. The Council says that it is from newness of attitudes, from self-denial and from the outpouring of charity that yearnings for unity arise and grow toward maturity. It is in this context that Vatican II repeats the words of Saint Paul: "I, then a prisoner in the Lord, urge you to live in a manner worthy of the call you have received" (Ephesians 4:1). These paragraphs urge us to acknowledge our sins according to the testimony of Saint John: "If we say, 'We have not sinned,' we make him a liar, and his word is not in us" (1 John 1:10). The Council tells us that this holds good also for sins against unity. For these, we must beg pardon of God and our separated brethren, just as we forgive those who trespass against us.

The following principle has far reaching effects for ecumenism and for introducing all the members of the Church into the ecumenical movement. It says that "all Christ's faithful should remember that the more purely they strive to live according to the Gospel, the more they are promoting, indeed exercising, Christian unity. For they can achieve depth and ease in strengthening mutual fraternal relations to the degree that they are united in profound communion with the Father, the Word and the Holy Spirit" (no.7).

Have we really yet understood what Vatican II has told us about promoting and indeed exercising ecumenism? Do we believe this? Look what the criterion is. Our mutual relations are strengthened (and is this not ecumenism?) to the extent that we are in profound communion with the Most Blessed Trinity. An extraordinary position!

The Church is telling us that ecumenism is God's work and the most effective way to approach it is *in communion with the Most Blessed Trinity.*

Change of Heart in Truth

The next paragraph codifies as it were this principle, saying: "This change of heart and holiness of life together with public and private prayer for the unity of Christians, should be regarded as the soul of the entire ecumenical movement and can rightly be called spiritual ecumenism." At this point it is crystal clear that if we are to engage in ecumenism, we must engage in it with pure hearts.

Vatican II goes on to speak about common prayer and the value of being gathered together, two or three in the name of Jesus. Common worship, however, is not a means to be used indiscriminately. In this there are two principles to be balanced and applied. One is that our worship, when we are speaking about the Eucharist, should signify the unity of the Church. It is meant to be the worship of those who are united. At the same time, worship provides the means of grace. For this reason, intercommunion is not the practice of the Church. There are exceptions (but they are indeed exceptions) when those who are not in full unity with the Church are permitted to receive Holy Communion. We see some of these exceptions in the way the Church deals with our separated Orthodox brethren.

In the Decree on Ecumenism we are encouraged as Catholics to acquire more adequate understanding of the doctrines of our separated brethren, as well as their history, their spiritual and liturgical life, their religious psychology and cultural background. Hence, meetings and dialogue are of great importance, but always *conversion and prayer are the soul of the ecumenical movement.* We are told in the Decree on Ecumenism that it is important to present our teaching correctly and that it is essential that our doctrine be presented in its entirety. Nothing, the Church tells us, is more foreign to the spirit of ecumenism than a false conciliatory approach, which harms purity of Catholic doctrine and obscures its genuine meaning.

Here we return to the great challenge launched by Pope John XXIII on the opening day of the Second Vatican

Council in which the Pope distinguishes between Catholic teaching and the way it is presented. He calls us to guard faithfully its content and at the same time to present ever more effectively its meaning. Theologians are encouraged to work together with our separated brethren and to act with love for truth, with charity and with humility. Collaboration among separated Christians is encouraged and it is hoped that this collaboration will promote the dignity of the human person, bring about peace, apply Gospel principles to the social life, advance the arts and sciences in a Christian spirit, and remove the afflictions of our times such as famine, natural disaster, illiteracy, poverty, lack of housing, and an unequal distribution of wealth.

Elements We Have in Common

The third and final chapter concerns the Churches and ecclesial communities separated from the Apostolic See of Rome. The Council speaks about the divisions of the East that go back all the way to the fifth century. It speaks about the divisions of the West, happenings referred to as *the Reformation*. It honors in a special way the Anglican Communion. The Council has many words of esteem and praise, encouraging Catholics to understand, venerate, preserve, and foster the exceedingly rich liturgical and spiritual heritage of the Eastern Churches.

Once again prayer and truthful dialogue are pointed out as means to realize the goal of Christian unity. In speaking about the separated Churches of the West, the Council emphasizes elements that we have in common. It speaks of a love, veneration and devotion for the Sacred Scriptures. It speaks of our common Baptism and how, in our separated brethren, the Christian way of life is nourished by faith in

Christ, by the grace of Baptism, by the hearing of God's word, by prayer and meditation, and in worship offered by communities to praise God. The faith of our separated brethren, which we are encouraged to recognize, bears fruit in praise and thanksgiving and is associated with a sense of justice and charity.

Vatican II in its Decree on Ecumenism recognizes the difference of *moral positions* at times and respectfully suggests that ecumenical dialogue could start with discussions concerning the application of the Gospel to moral questions. The Council urges the faithful to abstain from anything superficial. And, finally, the Council says that the holy task of reconciling all Christians in the unity of the one and only Church of Christ transcends human energies and abilities.

The Council, therefore, places its hope entirely in Christ's prayer for the Church, in the love of the Father for us, and in the power of the Holy Spirit. This brings us back once again to *the Most Blessed Trinity,* which is the model and exemplar of all Church unity.

VII

The Church and Non-Christian Religions: Respect for All Non-Christian Religions

In the City of St. Louis, there is an impressive Arch that stands close to the Mississippi River and is characteristic of the city. In the construction of that Arch, October 28, 1965, was an important date, because on that day, I am told, the two extremities of the Arch touched. That day was also the seventh anniversary of the election to the Papacy of Pope John XXIII. It was on his anniversary that the Second Vatican Council promulgated its Declaration on the Relationship of the Church to Non-Christian Religions.

The Latin title of the document was *Nostra Aetate:* "In Our Times." It began by saying: "In our times when everyday people are being drawn closer together and the ties between various peoples are being multiplied, the Church is giving deeper study to her relationship with non-Christian religions." Hence, the context of this decree is *a sign of the times,* of people being drawn closer together.

Already in the Dogmatic Constitution on the Church, the Council had spoken of the Church as being a sign, an instrument of intimate union with God and of the unity of all mankind. The Council was deeply interested in the unity of all mankind and made reference to the fact that all people have a single origin and one final goal, and both of these are God Himself.

Looking for Answers in Various Religions

Vatican II went on to explain that people look to the various religions for *answers to the profound mysteries about the human condition.* Who is man? What are the meaning and the purpose of life? What is goodness? And what is sin? What gives rise to our sorrows? Where does the path to true holiness lie? What is the truth about death, judgment, and retribution beyond the grave? What, finally, is that ultimate mystery which engulfs our being: where we come from, where our turning leads us?

With respect and esteem, the Council refers to various religions. It refers to *Hinduism* in its contemplation of the divine mystery. It evokes *Buddhism* in reference to a state of absolute freedom and supreme enlightenment. It states that the Catholic Church rejects nothing that is true and holy in any religion. The Council makes an even longer reference to *the Muslims,* evoking their acknowledgment of Jesus and the honor that they show to Mary, and also remembering the past and looking to the future.

Spiritual Patrimony Common to Christians and Jews

Vatican II then makes a particular reference to the spiritual bond that links the people of the New Covenant to Abraham's stock. The Council acknowledges receiving the revelation of the Old Testament through *the Jews.* The Church acknowledges the root of the good olive tree onto which the wild olive branches of the Gentiles have been grafted. In the Council, the Church recalls God's promises to the Fathers and the fact that the Apostles sprang from the Jewish people. The Council evokes the teaching of Saint Paul that the Jews still remain most dear to God because of the Fathers. In virtue of the spiritual patrimony common to Christians and Jews, the Council declares that it wishes to foster and recommend that *mutual understanding and respect,* which is the fruit, above all, of biblical and theological studies and of fraternal dialogues.

All of us recall what has been referred to as the Declaration on the Jews. The Council was very clear that the passion and death of Jesus cannot be blamed on all of the Jews living at the time of Christ, nor on the Jews of today. And, although the Church is the new people of God, *the Jews must not be presented as repudiated* by God. The Council insisted that catechetical instruction and the preaching of God's word should always be in harmony with the truth of the Gospel and the spirit of Christ.

Through the Council, the Church repudiated all persecutions against anyone. She deplored hatred, persecution, and *displays of anti-Semitism* directed against the Jews at any time and from any source. The Council also taught that Christ underwent His passion and death because of the sins of all people, so that all might attain salvation. Therefore, the Cross of Christ is the sign of God's all-embracing love.

The short decree concludes by saying that the Church rejects, as foreign to the mind of Christ, *any discrimination against people* or harassment of them because of their *race, color, condition of life,* or *religion.* The Church recommends that the faithful maintain good fellowship among the nations and, if possible, as far as in them lies, to keep peace with all people.

This document was certainly *in the spirit of Pope John XXIII,* who, as he convoked the Council, said these words:

"Finally to a world which is lost, confused and anxious under the constant threat of new frightful conflicts, the forthcoming Council must offer a possibility for all men of good will to turn their thoughts and their intentions toward peace, a peace which can and must above all come from spiritual and supernatural realities, from human intelligence and conscience, enlightened and guided by God, the Creator and Redeemer of humanity."

VIII

Divine Revelation:
The Word of God

Every morning during the Second Vatican Council, the
Book of the Gospels was carried in by a different Bishop
and the word of God was enthroned in St. Peter's Basilica.
And all the discussions that took place during the Second
Vatican Council took place *before the word of God.*

The Dogmatic Constitution on Divine Revelation
was one of the most important documents of the Second
Vatican Council. It is, in effect, the pronouncement of the
Second Vatican Council on the Bible, on Tradition, and
on God's revelation and man's response in faith. It is
good to keep in mind that the Constitution, besides its
opening words in the preface, is divided into six chapters:
1) Revelation itself, 2) Transmission of divine Revelation,
3) Divine inspiration and the interpretation of Sacred
Scripture, 4) the Old Testament, 5) the New Testament,
and 6) Sacred Scripture in the life of the Church.

Responding with Faith to the Deepest Truth about God

The Second Vatican Council began by assuring the world
that the Church *listens with reverence to the word of God* and
she proclaims it confidently. The Second Vatican Council
tells us that it is in continuity with the Council of Trent
and the First Vatican Council, and that it desires to set
forth authentic teaching about *divine revelation* and how it

is handed on in the Church. And the reason for desiring to hand on the teaching of divine revelation is that the whole world may believe and have hope and love.

In its first chapter on revelation itself, the Second Vatican Council explains to us how God chose to reveal Himself and to make known to us the hidden purpose of His will. Through this revelation, God has communicated to us the deepest truth about Himself and about our salvation. What is so wonderful about this revelation is that its final phase takes place in Jesus Christ. God spoke in many ways through the prophets, we are told in the Letter to the Hebrews, but last of all He has spoken to us through His Son Jesus Christ. *Jesus Christ is the fullest revelation of God.* He is indeed the Word of God, the Second Person of the Most Blessed Trinity who has become man.

As the Incarnate Word of God, Jesus Christ is our Mediator with the Father. He makes it possible for us who have received the Father's revelation to accept it in Him. Revelation itself requires that we respond to this act of God, that we respond to God's message that is incarnate in His Son, and that we do this by what Saint Paul calls *the obedience of faith.* This faith is the full submission of our intellect and our will to God. It is a free assent to the truth that God reveals. It is the free acceptance of the truth that is made incarnate in Jesus Christ. Centuries ago, Saint Thomas Aquinas gave us a beautiful definition of the act of faith. He tells us that it is an act of our intellect that assents to the divine truth, an act that is made under the command of our will and under the influence of God's grace. The response that all of us are called to give to divine revelation is, therefore, a gift of God.

From the Divine Wellspring to the Ends of the Earth

In the second chapter of the Dogmatic Constitution on Divine Revelation, the Council speaks to us about the way revelation is transmitted. Of great importance is the teaching that *sacred Tradition and Scripture form one sacred deposit of the word of God.* Both sacred Tradition and sacred Scripture come to us from the same divine wellspring, from the same divine source, which is God Himself who reveals. And coming from one source in two distinct ways, they constitute *one sacred deposit of the word of God.* And it is this word of God that is transmitted to the Church.

At this point, the Second Vatican Council explains to us that Christ our Lord, in whom the full revelation of God reaches completion, commissioned the Apostles to preach the Gospel to all people. Christ chose the Apostles for this particular purpose: to be His witnesses to the ends of the earth, to proclaim His Gospel, and, on the basis of God's revelation, to establish the Church in the power of the Holy Spirit throughout the world.

The Second Vatican Council goes on to explain to us that this plan of God was to be kept alive from generation to generation through the Bishops, who are the Successors of the Apostles and who continue the Apostles' teaching in the Church. The word of God, which is handed down from the Apostles, is expressed in a very special way in the inspired writings, in the Gospels, and in the other writings of the New Testament. But even as the Apostles hand down the message that they receive, the faithful are instructed to hold fast to what they have learned by word of mouth or by letter. Saint Paul emphasizes this in his Second Letter to the Thessalonians, where he says: "Stand firm and hold fast to the traditions that you were taught either by an oral statement or by a letter of ours" (2 Thessalonians

2:15). According to the Council, Sacred Scripture is the word of God consigned in writing under the inspiration of the Holy Spirit. Sacred Tradition hands on God's revelation entrusted to the Apostles by Christ and the Holy Spirit. And both sacred Tradition and sacred Scripture form but *one sacred deposit of the word of God committed to the Church.*

The task of authentically interpreting the word of God, whether written or handed on, has been entrusted exclusively to the Church. The Council makes clear that the teaching office in the Church is not superior to the word of God. It serves it by teaching faithfully only what has been handed on; it listens to the word of God devoutly, guarding it meticulously and explaining it faithfully with the help of the Holy Spirit. The teaching office of the Church draws from this single deposit of faith everything that it presents for belief as divinely inspired.

The Second Vatican Council in the Constitution *Dei Verbum* speaks repeatedly of *the Holy Spirit.* It is through the power of *the Holy Spirit* that the Tradition that comes from the Apostles develops in the Church. Over the years through the presence of the Holy Spirit there also occurs in the Church *a growth in the understanding* of those words and realities that have been handed down by the Apostles and their successors.

The Message of the Holy Spirit Communicated by Sacred Authors

In chapter three, after the Council had explained clearly *the two aspects of the single revelation of God,* it then dwells on Sacred Scripture itself, on *the divine inspiration of Sacred Scripture,* and on the *interpretation of Sacred Scripture.* This teaching makes special reference to the teaching of Pope

Pius XII, to the teaching of the First Vatican Council, to the teaching of Pope Leo XIII and to the teaching of Pope Benedict XV. The Council makes clear that the Books of Sacred Scripture have *God as their author* and that they have been handed on as such to the Church. With reference both to Pope Pius XII and to Pope Leo XIII, the Council tells us that, in composing the sacred books, God chose men. And while employed by Him they made use of their powers and abilities so that, with Him acting in them and through them, they were true authors and consigned to writing everything and only those things that God wanted.

Catholic doctrine, therefore, is very clear that the Sacred Scriptures have God as their author, and that the human authors—the sacred writers involved in the composition of the Sacred Scriptures—have communicated what the Holy Spirit wishes them to communicate. Therefore, the Books of Scripture must be acknowledged as teaching firmly, faithfully, and without error the truths that God desired to be in the Sacred Writings for the sake of our salvation.

The Council reminds us that Saint Paul had long since taught: "All scripture is inspired by God and is useful for teaching, for refutation, for correction, for training and righteousness so that the one who belongs to God may be competent, equipped for every good work" (2 Thessalonians 3:16–17).

In the richness of its teaching, the Second Vatican Council explains to us that we must examine "the literary forms of each part of Scripture. The truth of God's word is expressed in a variety of ways, depending on whether the text is history of one kind or another, or whether it is a text of prophecy, poetry or some other type of speech. It is very important for the interpreter to investigate what meaning the sacred writer intended to express and actually expressed in his contemporary literary form."

The Council tells us that, in interpreting the Sacred Scriptures, serious attention must be given to the content and the unity of the whole of Scripture. The living tradition of the whole Church must be taken into account. And in the final analysis, the interpretation of Sacred Scripture is subject to the judgment of the Church, which carries out the divine commission of guarding and interpreting the word of God.

The New Testament Hidden in the Old

Chapters four and five of the Constitution on Divine Revelation speak respectively about *the Old Testament* and *the New Testament.* It is pointed out that God is the inspirer and the author of both Testaments and that He has wisely arranged that the New Testament be hidden in the Old and that the Old be manifested in the New. The principal purpose of the Old Testament was to prepare for the coming of Christ and His messianic kingdom, to announce this coming by prophecy, and to indicate its meaning through various types. The Books of the Old Testament were then, according to the teaching of the Church, written under divine inspiration and remain permanently valuable, even though they contain some things that are incomplete and temporary.

The Council tells us clearly that among all the Scriptures, even those of the New Testament, the Gospels have a preeminence, and rightly so, for they are the principal witness of the life and teaching of Jesus Christ the Incarnate Word, our Savior.

The Church has always held and continues to hold that the four Gospels are of *apostolic origin*. The Church unhesitatingly asserts that the four Gospels faithfully hand on what Jesus Christ really did and taught for the eternal salvation of mankind. Besides the four Gospels, the New Testament contains the Epistles of Saint Paul and other apostolic writings composed under the inspiration of the Holy Spirit. In all of these writings the power of God is set forth for the salvation of all who believe.

The Scriptures and the Eucharist: Nourishment for the People of God

The final chapter of the Dogmatic Constitution on the Word of God is of extreme importance because it treats of Sacred Scripture in the life of the Church. The Council reminds us that *the Church has always venerated the Sacred Scriptures as she venerates the Body of the Lord.* The Scriptures and the Eucharist, in different ways, both constitute nourishment for the people of God. The Church regards the Scriptures together with sacred Tradition as the supreme rule of faith. The Council tells us that all the preaching of the Church must be nourished and ruled by the Sacred Scripture. How consistent it was with the purpose of the Council then, to see the beautiful Book of the Gospels always enthroned in St. Peter's Basilica as discussions took place about the Church and eternal salvation.

The Council reminds us that in the Sacred Books our Father in heaven meets His children with great love and speaks to them. And from the word of God the Church derives strength and energy.

The Second Vatican Council goes on record as asking for *easy access to the Sacred Scriptures for all the Christian faithful.* The Second Vatican Council highly recommended for the clergy, religious, and all the faithful frequent reading of the divine Scriptures by which they receive the excelling knowledge of Jesus Christ. This exhortation to diligent reading of the Sacred Scriptures on the part of all is an indication of the profound reverence with which the Second Vatican Council holds the word of God.

Back in 1893 Pope Leo XIII in his encyclical on the study of Sacred Scripture quoted at that time the words of Saint Jerome: "To be ignorant of the Scriptures is to be ignorant of Christ." This certainly applies to all the members of the Church."

The Second Vatican Council makes it clear that the reading of Sacred Scripture should be accompanied by *prayer.*

In order that all the faithful should have easy access to the Scriptures, the Council also expressed the hope that there would be *suitable and correct translations* made of the Sacred Scriptures into different languages and that these would be made especially from the original texts of Scripture. At the same time, in an attitude of ecumenical collaboration, the Second Vatican Council expressed the hope that the translations would be produced in cooperation with our separated brethren when possible.

The Study of Scripture: The Soul of Theology

The Ecumenical Council also encourages Catholics who are biblical scholars to continue energetically with the work they have begun.

Because of the preeminent position of the word of God in the Church, the Second Vatican Council envisioned so much of the renewal that it was promoting as being linked to the word of God. In particular, Vatican II said that sacred theology rests on the written word of God together with sacred Tradition as its primary and perpetual foundation. It asserted that theology is most powerfully strengthened and rejuvenated by the word of God, and that *the study of the Sacred Scriptures* is like *the soul of sacred theology.* The ministry of God's word includes pastoral preaching, catechetics, and all other Christian instruction among which the liturgical homily should have a place of special importance.

The final words of the Dogmatic Constitution on Divine Revelation draw our attention to the growth of the life of the Church that comes through constant participation in the Eucharist. At the same time, the Second Vatican Council expresses hope for a new surge of spiritual vitality from intensified veneration of God's word.

The Second Vatican Council has indeed launched a great challenge to the Church and to each one of us her members. It is a challenge of *increased Bible reading and Bible study.* It is a challenge of *increased veneration for the word of God* and also of *increased thanksgiving to God* for the great gift of His divine revelation. This revelation has come to us from one source, from God Himself, and it has come to us in two ways: by the written word and by sacred Tradition.

How fitting then are the honor, reverence, and profound veneration that the Second Vatican Council showed to the word of God exposed in the Book of the Gospels, recalling to all the Fathers of Vatican II and to the whole world that God's holy word remains forever.

IX

Religious Freedom:
The Dignity of Being Free

In the Cathedral Basilica of St. Louis, in the main dome, there is a magnificent mosaic that represents the Most Blessed Trinity at the moment of the Crucifixion of Jesus. The mosaic portrays Jesus hanging on the Cross. There are no nails, there are no cords that hold Him to the Cross; there is only His desire to offer up His life freely to the Father. At the same time there is the beautiful artistic image of the Father supporting His Son Jesus so that Jesus will not slip off the Cross. In other words, the idea is clear that Jesus, in His human nature, is exercising His great gift of freedom. And in this He finds His Father's approval and His Father's help. The mosaic actually furnishes us a very beautiful figure with which to reflect on *the freedom that was present in the human nature of Jesus.*

But this freedom is actually present in each one of us. It is a gift of God. When this freedom is directed to the choice of religion, it is known as *religious freedom.* And it is precisely this religious freedom that is the theme and title of a document of the Second Vatican Council.

For Vatican II, this freedom with which every human being is endowed is *an expression of the dignity of the human person.* And these words constitute in the Latin text the title of this document on religious freedom: *Dignitatis humanae.*

The Right of Individuals
and the Right of Communities

The document opens up by saying that in our contemporary world people are becoming ever more conscious of their own dignity, of their dignity as persons. It is in this way that the Second Vatican Council launches us into the whole question of religious freedom. The Declaration on Religious Freedom speaks about *the right of individuals* and *the right of communities* to social and civil freedom in matters of religion. The document is divided into two chapters: 1) The General Principle of Religious Freedom, and 2) Religious Freedom in the Light of Revelation.

Right away, in chapter one, Vatican II makes it clear that *the human person has a right to religious freedom.* And immediately the Council gives a summary of its teaching on this important topic. It states that "religious freedom means that all people must be immune from coercion, on the part of individuals or of social groups, and of any human power in such a way that, in matters of religion, no one is to be forced to act in a manner *contrary* to his or her beliefs. Nor is anyone to be restrained from acting *according* to his or her own beliefs, whether privately or publicly, whether alone or in association with others, within due limits."

The declaration also presents the context in which it is speaking. It says that the right to religious freedom has its foundation in the very dignity of the human person, as *this human dignity is known through the revealed word of God and by reason itself.*

At this point, the document makes reference to Pope John XXIII, to Pius XII, to Pius XI, and all the way back to Leo XIII, who wrote an encyclical on human liberty in 1888. Even as it makes reference to these former statements that help convey the teaching of the Church in regard to human dignity and religious freedom, the document itself presents conclusions that are indeed part of the wonderful development of doctrine that takes place in the Church continually under the direction and guidance of the Spirit of Truth, the Holy Spirit.

For the Church as Well as for Others

At the same time that the Church is adamant in requiring *religious freedom for herself,* she is also insistent in attributing *to others* the same religious freedom. There are many statements in the document that help us understand the final conclusions of Vatican II and its teaching on religious freedom. The Declaration states, for example, that the exercise of religion consists above all in internal, voluntary, and free acts whereby a human being sets the course of his life directly toward God. No merely human power can either command or prohibit acts of this kind. Another factor to be taken into account is the fact that the social nature of man himself requires that he should give external expression to his internal acts of religion, that he should participate with others in religion, and that he should profess his religion in a community. Freedom or immunity from coercion in religious matters also applies to this aspect of religious freedom. Religious bodies are a requirement of the social nature, both of man and religion itself. *Religious bodies have the right not to be hindered in their public teaching and witness* to the faith, whether by the spoken word or the written word. However this certainly does not include any coercion or undue persuasion—what we generally today call *proselytism.*

The *family* is a society, the most fundamental of societies, and it has the right freely under the guidance of the parents to live its religious life. The consequence of this is that government must acknowledge the right of parents to make a genuinely free choice of schools and of other means of education. Children cannot be forced to attend instruction or schools that are not in agreement with the religious belief of the parents. This happens and is unjust if a single system of education from which all religious formation is excluded is imposed upon all. Government has, as part of its essential duties, the role of protecting and promoting the inviolable rights of people. For this reason, *government must safeguard the religious freedom of all its citizens* and it must do this by just laws and other appropriate means.

The Second Vatican Council recognizes that circumstances can permit special legal recognition to be given in the constitutional order to one religious body. But at the same time, the right of all citizens and religious bodies to religious freedom must be recognized and made possible in practice.

Since *the right to religious freedom* is exercised in human society, its exercise *is subject to certain regulations and norms.* The use of all freedoms requires personal and social responsibility. In the exercise of their rights, individuals and social groups are bound by the moral law to have respect both for the rights of others and for their own duties toward others for the common welfare of all. Society has the right to defend itself against possible abuses that are committed under the pretext of freedom of religion.

Chapter two of the document speaks about religious freedom in the light of divine revelation. Here Vatican II points out that *the right to religious freedom has its foundation in the dignity of the human person.* It tells us that the requirements of this dignity have come to be more adequately known to human reason through centuries of experience, but that this doctrine of freedom has its roots in God's revelation. And, for this reason, Christians are bound to respect it all the more conscientiously.

Free Response to God

The Council does not hesitate to assert that one of the major tenets of Catholic doctrine is that *man's response to God in faith must be a free response.* No one, therefore, is to be forced to embrace the Christian faith against his or her own will. Vatican II asserts that this doctrine is contained in the word of God and that it was constantly proclaimed by the Fathers of the Church. The act of faith is by its very nature a free act. A person cannot give his or her adherence to God revealing Himself unless the Father draw that person to offer to God the reasonable and free submission of faith.

Therefore, in matters of religion, *all coercion is to be excluded.* Consequently, this principle of religious freedom makes a great contribution to the creation of an environment in which people can, without hindrance, be invited to the Christian faith and embrace it with their own free will and profess it effectively in their whole manner of living.

Vatican II makes the point that God calls people to serve Him and to serve Him according to His will in spirit and in truth. Hence, people are bound in conscience to do what God wants them to do, but they cannot be put under physical compulsion. God has consideration for the dignity of the human person and God wants man to say *yes,* but to say *yes* freely, that is, to exercise his freedom of religion.

In everything that Christ Himself did, His intention was to rouse faith in those listening to Him, to strengthen them in faith but not to exert coercion upon them. Jesus said: "He who believes and is baptized will be saved, but he who does not believe will be condemned" (Mark 16:16). The Apostles were taught by the word and the example of Christ. From the very beginning of the Church the disciples of Christ endeavored to convert people to faith in Christ, not by the use of coercion, but by the power of the word of God. The Apostles showed boldness and confidence in preaching the word of God, but they rejected weapons of coercion. Throughout the ages, the Church has accepted this doctrine of Christ. This does not prevent the Council from recognizing that, in the life of the people of God, through the vicissitudes of history, there have at times been ways of acting which were opposed to the spirit of the Gospel. Yet the doctrine of the Church has always stood firm that *no one is to be coerced into faith.*

Religious Freedom: A Sign of the Times

The Church claims freedom for herself in her own role as a spiritual authority established by Christ. The Church also claims freedom for herself in her role as a social entity with the right to live in society according to the precepts of the Christian faith. Both the Christian faithful and all people should possess the civil right not to be hindered in leading their lives in accordance with their conscience. In order to be faithful to God's command "Make disciples of all nations" (Matthew 28:19), the Catholic Church must work with urgency and concern for the spread of the word of God. It is the Church's duty to teach the truth about Christ Himself and to present those principles of the moral order that have their origin in human nature. In all her endeavors, however, the Church rules out any coercion while claiming *freedom for herself and other individuals and societies* to profess their religious beliefs in private and in public.

Vatican II notes that religious freedom has been declared to be a civil right in most constitutions and it is solemnly recognized in international documents, and yet there are forms of government which, while professing freedom of religious worship, are engaged in efforts to deter citizens from the profession of religion and to make life dangerous for religious communities.

The Council has in its own time recognized the globalization that is taking place in the world—nations coming together in ever closer unity, people of different cultures and religions being brought together in closer relationships. For this reason, the Council maintained for the good of all mankind that religious freedom be everywhere provided with an effective constitutional guarantee, and that respect be shown for the duty and right of the human being freely to lead his or her religious life in society.

Religious freedom for the Second Vatican Council *is a sign of the times.* It is a need of the human person. It is intimately linked to the demands of human dignity. It belongs to all people by reason of God's plan of creation and redemption. For Vatican II to respect the conscience of the human person in the matter of religion is to act in accordance with the teaching of the Church, with the example of Jesus and with the will of God.

X

Bishops: Called To Be Living Signs of Jesus Christ

To understand the role of the Bishop in the Church, according to the mind of the Second Vatican Council, we have to turn to the Decree on the Pastoral Office of Bishops in the Church. We must also look at the Dogmatic Constitution on the Church, chapter three, which treats the entire hierarchal structure of the Church: Bishops, priests and deacons. And it does so in the context of *the people of God.*

To understand Vatican II's view of the Bishop, it is good to look to the example of the two great Bishops of Rome who convoked and conducted the Second Vatican Council. The first one is Pope John XXIII and the second one is Pope Paul VI.

To understand the role of the Bishop in the Church, we should also include the example of Pope John Paul II. He was present for the entire Vatican Council and, in the providence of God, he was the chief implementer of Vatican II through all the years of his pontificate. His example as a Bishop and his teaching on the role of the Bishop are both excellent expressions of what the Second Vatican Council had in mind for the Bishops of the Church. This vision of Vatican II about the Bishop is faithfully continued today by Pope Benedict XVI.

In his First Letter, Saint Peter presents to us *our Lord Jesus Christ as the Shepherd and Bishop of our souls.*

This is the final and principal dimension of the figure of the Bishop as faithfully expressed by the Second Vatican Council.

To Make Present Our Lord Jesus Christ

One of the favorite texts of Pope John Paul II is found in the Dogmatic Constitution on the Church. It reads: "In the Bishops, whom the priests assist, the Lord Jesus Christ, the Supreme High Priest, is present in the midst of the believers" (no. 21). With these words, the Second Vatican Council has zeroed in on the spiritual role, *the essential role of the Bishop,* which is to *make present our Lord Jesus Christ,* to make Him present for the body of the faithful, to make Him present, together with the priests of the Church. This is indeed a magnificent role, a weighty charge and a beautiful plan that God has for His Church.

There are then many ways in which the Bishop together with the priests makes Christ present in the Church. There are many ways in which the episcopal ministry is exercised. We must reflect on some of these.

But first of all, let us remember, as the Letter to the Hebrews says, those who have been our leaders. Pope John XXIII appeared on the scene as a man sent from God. He exercised the role of the episcopacy in its highest form, as Bishop of Rome. He made incarnate the kindness, the love of Christ in His own flesh. John XXIII was known as the good Pope, *il Papa buono.* His Christ-likeness was immediately recognized by the people of God. They sensed what Jesus was like, because His chief representative was so kind, so authentic, so gentle, so strong.

John XXIII, as Bishop of Rome, was succeeded by Paul VI who gave another expression of gentleness and kindness, of authentic humanity to the role of the episcopacy as it is exercised at its supreme level in the Vicar of Christ for the universal Church.

Although I was in Rome for a good portion of the pontificate of John XXIII, I did not know him personally. I did have, however, the personal experience of spending years in close contact with Pope Paul VI. I had the great privilege of working with him and for him, of assisting him in the Vatican Secretariat of State. For the last eight and a half years of his life, I was honored to be his English-language translator. And, through constant contact with him, I was able to admire how he exemplified the role of the Shepherd and Bishop of our souls and how, through him, our Lord Jesus Christ was present in the midst of the community of believers.

With the Pastoral Love of Christ

Like John XXIII, Paul VI was a faithful and authentic representation of the kindness, the love, the goodness of Christ. The pastoral love of Paul VI was worthy of being identified with the *pastoral love of Christ* as Shepherd and Bishop of our souls.

Permit me to give you just one example. Some time in late January or early February 1977, while I was in the service of the Secretariat of State, Monsignor Macchi, the Secretary of Pope Paul VI, called me one day and said that the Holy Father would like to see me in the evening. I went to his private quarters on the third floor of the Apostolic Palace. The Holy Father spoke to me about a pastoral matter that he had at heart. And then, when our meeting was over, I proceeded to say goodbye to the Holy Father and to go toward the door of his office. But before I could leave, he stopped me and asked me how Paul was. Paul was my brother. The Holy Father had remembered his name. It was easy for him to do so since it was his own. I had asked the Pope to pray for Paul some time before, because he was very sick. As a matter of fact, he was dying of cancer. He was married, the father of twelve children and he was fifty years old. The Holy Father had four questions: How is Paul? How is his wife holding up? How are the children doing? And finally: What can I do? It was a very moving experience, because here was the chief Bishop of the Catholic Church concerned with a billion Catholics, but in the tenderness of his pastoral role concerned also about one human being, about Paul, and concerned about another human being, his wife, Louise, and about their children. Like the Good Shepherd, he was able to think of individuals without denying his pastoral care to the entire flock spread throughout the world. I offer this as an example that gives an insight on how the role of Bishop was exercised by Pope Paul VI with extraordinary pastoral love.

The same can be said of Pope John Paul II, whom I also was privileged to serve for many years and in different ways. He always exemplified the charity of Christ and always was driven by the pastoral good of God's people to make every effort, so that the word of God was preached to them in their own language. And this zeal and pastoral love prompted him to continue the role that Paul VI inaugurated with great zeal of traveling around the world. Paul VI traveled to all the continents: to Africa, to Latin America, in Europe. He came to the United States, to the United Nations. He went to Australia and to Asia. He visited parishes of Rome and dioceses throughout Italy.

And subsequently John Paul II, who referred to Paul VI a his "spiritual father," kept alive that legacy and through his dynamism and personal energy was able to fulfill in even greater measure the pastoral role exercised by Paul VI.

John Paul II went from continent to continent, and back again, proclaiming Jesus Christ. And in *proclaiming Jesus Christ,* he proclaimed *the dignity and worth of every human being.* He did this with great trust in Christ, the Shepherd and Bishop of our souls, and with great confidence in Mary the Mother of Jesus. His pontificate was a wonderful unfolding of the teaching of Vatican II on what a Bishop should be, what a Bishop should do. On the day after his election to the papacy, Pope Benedict XVI confirmed his determination to continue to implement the Second Vatican Council.

Obviously, it is not necessary to present only Popes as examples of Bishops who are faithful to the ideals of the Second Vatican Council. There have been many other Bishops before, during and after Vatican II who have exemplified splendidly the qualities outlined by Vatican II. Bishops like Charles Borromeo have been examples for centuries of a pastoral ideal that is lived in holiness of life and in generous collaboration with priests and other Bishops.

In the Context of the People of God

The context for the consideration of the pastoral office of the Bishop is found in chapter two of the Dogmatic Constitution on the Church *(Lumen Gentium).* Here the Church is presented as the People of God; here the Bishop's role is understood according to God's plan. Only after Vatican II has presented the entire picture of the Church in her mystery and in her various categories is the hierarchical structure of the Church presented. And after this there are presented the role of the laity, the universal call of everyone to holiness, and the role of religious.

The Decree on the Pastoral Office of Bishops is linked to the presentation of chapter three of *Lumen Gentium.* The Decree was passed with 2,322 votes, of which 2,319 were positive, two were negative, and one vote was void. The teaching certainly represents a magnificent consensus of the Bishops present at Vatican II. The decree begins by situating the mystery of the episcopacy in the context not only of the Church, but also of *the Most Blessed Trinity.* Jesus was sent by His Father, and Jesus sent the Apostles, conferring on them the Holy Spirit so that they might continue His mission.

The preface to the Decree points out that in Christ's Church *the Roman Pontff is the Successor of Peter* to whom Christ entrusted the feeding of His sheep and lambs. Hence, it is clear from the beginning that the Roman Pontiff enjoys supreme, full, immediate, and universal authority over the Church. He is truly, in the mystery of the Church, the pastor of all the faithful, including the Bishops, and His mission is to provide for the universal Church. It is interesting to note that every decree of the Second Vatican Council was signed first by the Pope and then by the individual Bishops. Each one put down his title. Pope Paul VI signed all the documents of Vatican II with the solemn title that is traditionally used in the signing of conciliar documents and dogmatic definitions. He signed: "I, Paul, Bishop of the Catholic Church." He is the only one who is Bishop of the universal Church, but he is not the only Bishop. The fact that he has this special role of service to the universal Church and that he has the title of Vicar of Christ for the universal Church does not preclude the fact that the other Bishops of the Church have also been appointed by the Holy Spirit. They are successors of the Apostles and, together with the Bishop of Rome and under his authority, they have been commissioned to be true and authentic teachers of the faith. They have been called to sanctify and to govern the faithful.

And all together *the Bishops are united in a college* or episcopal body. And this episcopal body is considered by Vatican II to be the successor of the College of the Apostles. Together with the head of the College, who is the Roman Pontiff and never without him, this body is the subject of supreme and full power over the universal Church. But this power can be exercised only with the consent of the Roman Pontiff.

This is the mystery of the Church as presented in its first hierarchical dimension. The Bishops are truly the successors of the Apostles. They are truly authentic pastors of their local Churches, but always in communion with the Bishop of Rome and with all those other Bishops who are in communion with the Bishop of Rome.

Father, Pastor, and Servant

One of the consequences of being a member of the college of Bishops is that each individual Bishop, together with his brother Bishops, must be concerned with *the needs of the entire Church*. Every Bishop is concerned with the needs of the people of God everywhere, and the greatest of all needs is the need to be evangelized. The solidarity of Bishops throughout the world is called episcopal communion and it has a universal character.

The Decree on Bishops explains what a diocese is, that it is a portion of God's people entrusted to a Bishop to be shepherded by him with the cooperation of his priests. Each diocese is a particular Church in which the one holy, Catholic, and apostolic Church of Christ is truly present and operative. And the Bishop is truly t*he father, pastor,* and *servant* of this particular or local Church. In this Church he exercises his duty of proclaiming the Gospel, proclaiming Jesus Christ. He is called to present Christian doctrine in a manner adapted to the needs of the time, to show special concern for the poor and those in need, to foster dialogue with members of society. The Bishop is the chief catechist in the diocese.

The Bishop is likewise called *to sanctify.* He offers the Eucharist for the people of God and he is the principal dispenser of the mysteries of God. He governs, promotes, and guards the entire liturgical life of the Church committed to him and he does this in union with the Holy See. He is charged with leading the flock to Christian perfection and, therefore, he should be mindful of his obligation to give an example of holiness through charity, humility, and simplicity of life.

Vatican II is very clear in asserting that, as father and pastor, the Bishop stands in the midst of his people as *one who serves.* He is challenged to know his sheep and to be a true father to them, excelling in the spirit of love and concern for all. The Bishop is called to deal lovingly with those who are separated from the Church. He is called to foster ecumenism as it is understood by the Church and to have at heart the welfare of those who are not baptized, so that they too may experience the charity of Christ. Every group of people deserves the solicitude of the Bishop. Vatican II recalls the migrants, the exiles, the refugees, the seamen, airplane personnel, gypsies, and other significant groups.

The Decree of Bishops emphasizes the relationship between *the Bishop and his diocesan priests,* stating that the relationship should rest above all on the bonds of supernatural charity, so that the harmony of the will of the priests with that of the Bishop will render their pastoral activity more fruitful. All priests have a special role of collaboration with the Bishop, but pastors are singled out in a special way as being entrusted with the care of souls in a certain part of the diocese under the Bishop's authority. Pastors and associates are called to fulfill their pastoral duties in such a way that parishioners and parish communities really experience being members of the diocese and the universal Church.

Religious priests, Vatican II says, are consecrated for the office of the priesthood so that they may be prudent cooperators of the episcopal order. They share in the care of souls and carry out works of the apostolate under the authority of the Bishops. A well-ordered cooperation is to be encouraged between various religious communities, and between them and the diocesan clergy. All of this depends, according to Vatican II, on a supernatural attitude of hearts and minds, an attitude rooted and founded upon charity.

Synod of Bishops for the Universal Church

The Second Vatican Council fully recognized the institution of *the Episcopal Conference.* This institution is given a great role to play in the life of the Church. The Decree on Bishops had expressed the hope that the Holy Father would establish a Synod of Bishops that would act to some extent in the name of the entire Catholic episcopate and show that all the Bishops share in responsibility for the universal Church. At the beginning of the fourth session of Vatican II, on September 15, 1965, Pope Paul VI accepted this suggestion and announced the institution of the Synod of Bishops. The Synod of Bishops has proved to be an extraordinary instrument of collegiality and service to the universal Church.

Of special interest is the Synod that was held in 1997 and was followed in January 1999 by the Post-Synodal Apostolic Exhortation *Ecclesia in America.* The theme of this Synod was *Encounter with the Living Jesus Christ: The Way to Conversion, Communion, and Solidarity in America.* Similar Synods have been held for Europe, Asia, Oceania, and Africa. Synods were also held on many individual topics such as the priesthood, religious life, the laity, the family, reconciliation, and penance. All of these synods, with their teaching, represent an enormous fruit of the Second Vatican Council. The Cardinal who conducted the Synods for years as the Secretary General was Cardinal Jan Schotte. He had lived in the United States and frequently visited our country.

Some years ago in the *Ad limina* visit of the Bishops of the United States, Pope John Paul II spoke at length about the ministry of Bishops (cf. Address of September 5, 1983). He summarized the ministry of Bishops in these words: "To understand the Church of the Incarnate Word, in which all grace is dispensed through the sacred humanity of the Son of God, is to understand how important it is for every Bishop in his own humanity to be *a living sign of Jesus Christ* (cf. *Lumen Gentium,* no. 21). We who are invested with the mission of the Good Shepherd have to make him visible to our people. We must respond in a specific way to the cry that comes from every corner of the world: 'We wish to see Jesus' (John 12:21). And the world wants to see him in us." He went on to say, drawing the consequences of what it means to be a living sign of Jesus Christ: "It is evident in all of this that the Bishop, a living sign of Jesus Christ, must vindicate to himself the title and accept the consequences of the fact that he is, with Jesus Christ, *a sign of contradiction.* Despite every dutiful effort to pursue the dialogue of salvation, the Bishop must announce to the young and old, to the rich and poor, to the powerful and weak, the fullness of truth which sometimes irritates and offends even if it always liberates. The justice and holiness that he proclaims are born of this truth (cf. Ephesians 4:24). The Bishop is aware that he must preach 'Jesus Christ and him crucified' (1 Corinthians 2:2), the same Jesus who said: 'If anyone would come after me, let him deny himself and take up his cross and follow me' (Matthew 16:24)."

At the end of his discourse, speaking to the American Bishops, the Holy Father said: "There is no deeper meaning in our lives as Bishops than to be *living signs of Jesus Christ!*" Certainly, this is what Vatican II was striving to communicate.

XI

Priests: Set Apart
in the Midst of God's People

Pope John Paul II was asked on more than one occasion what the greatest joy was in his life as Pope. The Holy Father responded that the greatest joy and privilege was to be able, like every Catholic priest throughout the world, *to celebrate the Eucharist.* Although he was Pope, the Bishop of Rome and visible head of the universal Church, his greatest joy was to be able to offer Mass.

The Second Vatican Council dedicated a document to the ministry and life of priests. It is known by its Latin title, *Presbyterorum Ordinis.* This document is divided into three chapters: 1) the Priesthood and the Mission of the Church, 2) the Ministry of Priests, and 3) the Life of Priests.

In the Decree on the Priesthood the nature of the priesthood is clearly linked with the sacred power of the priestly order *to offer sacrifice* and *to forgive sins.* Vatican II presents the priesthood as being conferred by a special sacrament through which priests are marked by the anointing of the Holy Spirit with a special character and are configured to Christ the Priest in such a way that they can act in the person of Christ the Head. Priests participate in the office of the Apostles and God gives them the grace to be ministers of Jesus Christ among the people.

Leading God's Family through Christ and in the Spirit to the Father

The priests shoulder a great part of the sacred task of the Gospel. The mission of the priesthood involves *gathering together the People of God by the proclamation of the Gospel* and enabling them to present their own spiritual sacrifices to the Father in union with the Sacrifice of Christ, who is the one Mediator.

Vatican II tells us that the ministry of priests takes its start from the Gospel message and derives its power and force from the Sacrifice of Christ. In the words of the Letter to the Hebrews the priests of the New Testament, like those of the Old, are "taken from among men." They are called to offer gifts and sacrifices for sins, and the gifts and sacrifices they offer are *the Sacrifice of Christ's Body and Blood.* In order that they may fulfill their vocation, priests are, in a certain sense, set apart in the midst of God's people, not in order to be separate from God's people, but only to be totally dedicated to the work for which the Lord has raised them up. Priests share the human condition. They have to offer the Sacrifice of Christ for their own sins as well as for the sins of the people. They are called to cultivate all the natural and supernatural virtues. The ministry of priests is beautifully outlined in this decree of Vatican II.

Priests are presented as *co-workers with their Bishops. Their primary duty is the proclamation of the Gospel.* We are told that in this way priests fulfill the Lord's command to go into the whole world and preach the Gospel to every creature. The proclamation of the Gospel is in no way separated from the sacramental proclamation of the death and resurrection of the Lord. In the Mass these two aspects of proclamation are inseparably linked. The Decree tells us that the other sacraments, as well as every ministry of the Church and every work of the apostolate, are linked with the Eucharist and directed toward it.

The high point of the Gospel's proclamation takes place in *the Eucharistic Sacrifice.* Vatican II tells us that "the Eucharist shows itself to be the source and summit of the whole work of evangelization" (no. 5). Priests are called upon to instruct the faithful to offer to God the Father, in the Sacrifice of the Mass, the Divine Victim, who is Jesus Christ, and to join to this the offering of their own lives.

Priests extend to the different hours of the day the praise and thanksgiving of the Eucharistic celebration by reciting *the Divine Office,* which is composed to such a great extent of the word of God.

Vatican II insists that priests exercise the office of Christ the Head and Shepherd. They gather God's family together in unity and lead it through Christ and in the Spirit to God the Father. They exercise spiritual power that is given to them for the building up of the Church. The priest is called upon to be concerned for all people and yet the Council enumerates various categories that need his ministry in a particular way—the poor and the lowly, the youth, married people and parents, religious, the sick and the dying. The office of the priest is not confined to the care of individuals but is also extended to the formation of a *genuine Christian community.*

So many of our priests find deep joy and fulfillment in their service to their Christian community, which, for so many of them, is the parish. Vatican II reminds us that no Christian community, however, can be built up unless it has its basis and center in the celebration of the Most Holy Eucharist.

Education in the spirit of community must begin with the Eucharist and it must lead people to works of charity, prayer, missionary activity, and Christian witness. In all of this, priests are *heralds of the Gospel* and *shepherds of the Church.* Priests and Bishops share in the one priesthood and ministry of Christ, and the very unity of their consecration and mission requires that they be united. Liturgical concelebration of priests with their Bishop has this deep significance. At every Mass, however, priests openly acknowledge that they celebrate the Eucharistic action in union with the Episcopate. For Bishops, the priests are *brothers, sons, counselors, friends, and necessary helpers* in the task of teaching, sanctifying, and nourishing the people of God.

In Holiness, Continued Formation, and Consultation

The document on the priesthood goes on to speak about the responsibility of the Bishop in regard to the material and especially the spiritual welfare of his priests. The Bishop is responsible for *the holiness of his priests.* For this reason, *the continued formation of priests* is very important. *Consultation* of the priests is likewise very important, and this is the principle that inspired the Council to establish what has become *the presbyteral council,* which assists the Bishop in the government of the diocese.

By reason of their ordination priests are united among themselves in an intimate *sacramental brotherhood,* forming one presbyterate with the Bishop. Whether they are engaged in parochial or supra-parochial ministry— whatever their particular work—they are all *co-workers with the Bishop* in the same ministry of Christ.

Priests are asked to be solicitous for other priests—those who are sick, afflicted, over-burdened with work, lonely, exiled from their homeland, or suffering persecution.

Vatican II asks for priests to be safeguarded from the dangers that arise from loneliness, and is therefore enthusiastic about fostering some kind or other of *community* life among priests. This may mean a shared roof, where this is feasible, or a common table, or frequent and regular gatherings. Circumstances vary greatly in different dioceses.

With the Encouragement and Love of the Faithful

Vatican II calls upon priests to exercise their role as father and teacher among the people of God. It insists that in the midst of the people of God priests are brothers among their brothers and sisters and all those who have been baptized. For this reason, priests are encouraged to promote *the dignity of the laity* and they are to acknowledge the multiple charisms of the laity. It is very edifying to see how the vast majority of our priests are deeply committed to this ministry and how they recognize that their own lives of service are so intimately intertwined with the well-being of the laity.

Vatican II spells out so many different activities of the priests who lead the people to the unity of charity. They are defenders of the truth of the Gospel. They are committed to those who have fallen away from the sacraments and perhaps from the faith. They are involved in the Church's activities on ecumenism, and they are called to be solicitous also for those who do not recognize Christ as their Savior.

The Second Vatican Council speaks to the lay faithful encouraging them to love and support their priests. We know that people do this by intuition and by grace.

They help priests to overcome difficulties and to be able to fulfill their duties more faithfully.

In the recent times of crisis the people of God have shown great wisdom in being able to distinguish between *the serious sins of individual priests* and *the faithful ministry of so many others*. One of the factors that makes the sexual abuse of minors by priests so grave is that it is so blatantly opposed to the meaning of their service and so contrary to the confidence that has been placed in them by minors and their parents.

The final reflection of the second chapter on the Ministry of Priests draws attention to the fact that priests by their ordination are called to have at heart the care of all the Churches. Every priestly ministry shares in the universality of the mission entrusted by Christ to His Apostles. Although only a restricted percentage of priests are destined for missionary activity and other special ministries in the universal Church, nevertheless the spirit of *universality* and *globalization* is part of the priestly vocation. At the same time, priests are reminded of the need to promote priestly vocations. Priests must be zealous in helping stir up in the hearts of young men a desire to share in the priestly ministry. Obviously, *the example* of true and authentic priestly dedication and conduct is an important part in inviting young people to the service of Christ's priesthood.

Chapter three on the Life of Priests is very explicit in indicating that the priestly call is a *call to perfection*. The Council speaks about it as a new way in which priests are consecrated to God by the reception of Holy Orders. It also states that "priestly holiness itself contributes very greatly to a fruitful fulfillment of the priestly ministry" (no. 12).

Priestly holiness is beautifully presented in Vatican II not only as being a *requirement* for priestly service, but

also as being *nourished and perfected by priestly ministry itself.*
At the same time, the Council urges priests to adopt the
means of holiness that are linked to their ministry.

The Eucharistic Sacrifice:
Center and Root of Priestly Life

Priests are encouraged every day to read and listen to *the
word of God.* Vatican II is especially clear in stating that
"priests fulfill their chief duty in the mystery of the Eucharistic
Sacrifice. In it the work of our redemption continues to be
carried out. For this reason priests are strongly urged to
celebrate Mass every day, for, even if the faithful are unable
to be present, it is an act of Christ and the Church" (no. 13).

And so it happens, according to Vatican II, that if
our priests unite themselves with the act of Christ, at the
same time they offer their whole selves every day to God.
In the same way they are joined with the love of Christ
when they administer His sacraments. Such is especially the
case when they show themselves entirely and always ready
to offer *the Sacrament of Penance* as often as the faithful
reasonably request it.

In the recitation of the Divine Office, they lend their
voice to the Church as she perseveres in prayer with Christ,
who lives always to make intercession for us. The Council
has a very important reflection on *the pastoral role of the
priest.* It tells us that, by assuming the role of the Good
Shepherd, priests find *in the very exercise of pastoral love the
bond of priestly perfection,* and that this will unify their lives
and activities. How consoling this is for so many of our
priests who work so hard and are constantly aware of so
many things that they are called upon to do for the good of
the faithful, while trying to maintain serenity and find the

appropriate time for prayer. They are greatly encouraged by the Council to know that, even as they exercise pastoral love, Christ is bringing to fulfillment in them the bond of priestly perfection.

The Council then says so clearly and distinctly that this pastoral love in the life of priests flows mainly from *the Eucharistic Sacrifice* and that this Eucharistic Sacrifice is therefore *the center and root of the whole priestly life.* The Council makes it clear also that to penetrate into the mystery of Christ the priest must be living a life of prayer.

The Council points out a special need in the priestly ministry to maintain hierarchical communion with the whole body. Obedient collaboration with the Bishop, the Pope, and the universal Church is a part of priestly existence.

Vatican II has a special word of commendation and insistence on the value and meaning of *celibacy* in the Latin rite. The Council exhorts priests to trust in God's grace in order to fulfill a commitment freely undertaken, but also to hold fast to it magnanimously, wholeheartedly and faithfully. In the life of the Church, this is certainly the hour for priests to rededicate themselves with absolute integrity to the celibacy they have vowed.

The lay faithful, who experience their own temptations and have their own obstacles in Christian discipleship, need to have the faithful example of priests as an encouragement in their own struggle for integrity and perfection. To support priests in their priestly life the Council invites them to turn to *the word of God,* to *the repeated sacramental act of Penance,* and to *a personal devotion to the Most Holy Eucharist.* Here priests are offered daily conversation with Christ the Lord.

Sustained in Joy, Never Alone!

The Council is also clear in pointing to Mary as the model of docility in the life of the priest. The Council actually enjoins a great deal on priests and asks that a great deal be done for priests to sustain them in their vocation. And both of these aspects are a continuing challenge to the individual priest and to the Church as a whole.

What comes through clearly in Vatican II is the desire of the Church to encourage priests to be faithful to their ministry and to support priests in every way possible so that they may be effective ministers to God's people and fulfill their indispensable role in the Church.

The Council concludes its reflections, exhorting the priests to joy in their priestly life, and assuring them that in the midst of difficulties and challenges *they are never alone.* They are encouraged to devote themselves to their ministry, *trusting in the Lord Jesus.* Their partnership is wide and extensive. It embraces their brother priests and indeed all the faithful of the world.

The final message of the Second Vatican Council to priests is to encourage them in the words of Jesus: "Take courage I have conquered the world" (John 16:33). And finally in this context of trust and confidence, Vatican II in its own expression gives "most loving thanks to all the priests of the world" (no. 22).

XII

Priestly Formation:
For Faithfulness and Service

Vatican II was convinced that *the deeply desired renewal* of the whole Church depends to a great extent on *the ministry of priests,* which is animated by the spirit of Christ. And the vital ministry of priests is, in turn, linked with *the priestly formation* that is given to candidates for the priesthood. And, so, the Second Vatican Council turned its attention to the important question of forming seminarians.

The Decree entitled *Optatam Totius* was signed by Pope Paul VI and the Bishops of the Church on October 28, 1965, the seventh anniversary of the election of John XXIII as Supreme Pontiff. The Decree begins by dedicating an entire chapter, which in effect is only a few sentences, to the question of the adaptation of priestly formation to individual countries.

Obviously so much of the content of priestly formation is common to every culture and every country, but nevertheless the circumstances of individual nations or particular rites require that there be an appropriate program of priestly formation in different places. The United States' Bishops have worked hard in presenting a priestly formation program that is precisely that—a program that reflects and incorporates the demands of the Second Vatican Council and is appropriate for the United States of America.

Everyone Included in Fostering Vocations

Before considering the actual question of priestly formation, the Decree examines the question of *fostering vocations*. Here it expresses the conviction that *the entire Christian community must be involved* in this important work. This includes *families* and *parishes*, it includes *young people* themselves, it includes *teachers* and *Catholic associations*. *Every priest* should manifest the zeal of an apostle in fostering vocations. A partnership in this cause spans the people of God and shares responsibility with everyone.

The Council draws attention to the importance of *prayer* and *mortification*. It speaks about *pastoral activity on behalf of vocations*, and mentions vocational *organizations* that foster this important goal in the Church. The Church is very proud of the efforts that are made by individuals and groups. The Church is very proud, for example, of the dedication of *Serra International*, which has been working for years in the promotion of vocations and has now spread to many countries of the world. What is so attractive in Serra International is the fact that laypeople who have their own vocation in the Church realize the importance for the entire Body of the Church to have holy priests and they are willing to spend themselves and exert great energy in persevering prayer and action to assist the Church in fostering these vocations.

The Council, in the second chapter of this document, takes note of the role of *minor seminaries*, realizing that these institutions require special attention and special direction. Although it is not mentioned explicitly in the Decree, the treatment of minor seminaries takes into account the principle that God Himself is free to call those whom He wants when He wants. The institution of the minor seminary gives to young people the opportunity to follow God's call when they perceive it, although it is obvious that the formation of the vast majority of seminarians begins at a later date.

Chapter three of the document goes into the question of *major seminaries* and the challenge that is before them to help train students who will develop into true shepherds of souls after the model of our Lord Jesus Christ. The goal of the seminary is clearly stated as directed toward *preparing men for the pastoral ministry.*

The Council points out how much the training of seminarians depends to a great extent on suitable teachers, directors, and professors. Here Vatican II goes back to cite the 1935 encyclical of Pius XI, *Ad Catholici Sacerdotii*, in which that Pope challenges the Bishops to put excellent priests in the work of seminary training. The same need exists today for excellent priests and laypeople in this work.

Spiritual, Doctrinal, and Pastoral Formation

The Council is adamant that necessary standards must always be firmly maintained, even if there exists a regrettable shortage of priests. Vatican II is convinced that God will not allow His Church to lack priests, if worthy candidates are admitted and unsuited ones are directed to other activities.

In treating, in chapter four, spiritual formation in seminaries, the Council expresses a conviction that spiritual formation is to be closely linked with *doctrinal and pastoral training.* It has a beautiful reference to the Most Blessed Trinity when it says that "the spiritual director should help seminarians learn to live in familiar and *constant companionship with the Father through Jesus Christ His Son in the Holy Spirit.*" Seminarians are to be trained to look for Christ in many places—in *the word of God,* in *the Eucharist,* in *the*

Divine Office, in *the Bishop*, in *the people* to whom they are sent, especially t*he poor, the young, the sick, the sinful*, and *the unbelieving*. The spiritual formation of seminarians includes devotion to our Blessed Mother—the Mother of Jesus and the Mother of His Church. The ideal to be inculcated into the seminarians is to live according to the Gospel and to grow in faith, hope, and charity.

Seminarians should understand very plainly that they are not called to dominate others or to receive honors, but to give of themselves in *obedience* and *humble living*. In being carefully trained for priestly celibacy, seminarians must be duly aware of the duties and dignity of Christian marriage. They are to be taught the dangers with which their chastity will be confronted and they are to be challenged in growth and maturity. Something that is very relevant to the particular demands of the present day is the conviction expressed by the Council that the norms of Christian education are to be maintained and complemented by the latest findings in sound *psychology* and *pedagogy*. It insists that there be a due degree of *human maturity* attested chiefly by *an emotional stability* and an ability to make *proper judgments*.

The *human qualities* that are highly regarded among people and speak well of a minister of Christ are to be cultivated. "Such are sincerity of heart, a constant concern for justice, fidelity to one's word, courtesy of manner, restraint and kindliness in speech" (no. 11).

The Council indicated the need for the revision of ecclesiastical studies and it gave detailed instructions in this regard. It spoke about *philosophy* and *theology*, insisting that students accurately draw Catholic doctrine from *divine revelation*, understand that doctrine profoundly, and nourish their own spiritual lives with it. In addition, they must be able to proclaim it, unfold it, and defend it in their priestly ministry.

Sacred Scripture is presented as *the soul of all theology* and in this Vatican II quotes Pope Leo XIII in his encyclical of 1893 on Sacred Scripture, called *Providentissimus Deus.* The Council speaks, in turn, about *dogmatic and moral theology*, about *canon law* and *history*, about *sacred liturgy*, and about *the study of the Fathers* of the East and the West. An appeal is made to students to search for solutions to human problems in the light of revelation and apply eternal truths to changing conditions of human affairs, communicating such truths in a manner suited to the people of our time. Once again we remember Pope John XXIII's Address on the opening day of Vatican II where he explained the distinction between *the content of the faith* and *the manner appropriate for its presentation.*

The Council is very much aware of the need to promote pastoral training and it does this in chapter six of the document. Seminarians are to receive careful instruction in *the art of guiding souls.* They should be directed to the promotion of dialogue and taught to open their hearts in a spirit of charity to various circumstances of human need. They are to be taught to use the helps that *pedagogy, psychology*, and *sociology* can offer. During the course of their studies, seminarians are to be introduced into pastoral practice under the guidance of people experienced in pastoral matters. In all of this, they must keep in mind the surpassing excellence of supernatural means.

The Council terminates by drawing attention to the fact that priestly training should be pursued and completed even after the seminary course of studies is finished. This norm is of great importance and experience teaches that priests not only need this *continuing education* but also are encouraged, uplifted, and sustained by it.

To Incarnate in Earthen Vessels the Good Shepherd's Love

Like other documents of the Second Vatican Council, this Decree on Priestly Formation has been providentially implemented by a Synod of Bishops. The Synod of 1990 was dedicated to *the formation of priests in the circumstances of the present day*. It culminated in the publication, on March 25, 1992, of the Post-Synodal Apostolic Exhortation of Pope John Paul II, *Pastores Dabo Vobis*. This Exhortation has, to a great extent, spelled out and amplified the already providential teaching of Vatican II. It has examined in more detail the challenges facing priestly formation, the nature and mission of the ministerial priesthood, the spiritual life of the priest, the priestly vocation and the Church's pastoral work, the formation of candidates for the priesthood, and the ongoing formation of priests. It is all this conciliar and post-synodal teaching that gives us such confidence today that the Church truly possesses accurate and effective instruments for forming the priests of our time and for assisting them to meet the challenges of their priestly life and ministry.

In bringing his post-synodal exhortation and challenge to a close, Pope John Paul II expressed these thoughts to both seminarians and priests: "I turn my thoughts to all aspirants to the priesthood, to seminarians and to priests who in all parts of the world—even in the most difficult and dramatic conditions, but always with the joyous struggle to be faithful to the Lord and to serve his flock unswervingly— are offering their lives daily in order that faith, hope and charity may grow in human hearts and in the history of the men and women of our day. . . . Dear brother priests, you do this because our Lord himself with the strength of his Spirit has called you to incarnate in the earthen vessels of your simple lives the priceless treasure of his Good Shepherd's love.

"In communion with the Synod Fathers and in the name of all the Bishops of the world and of the entire community of the Church I wish to express all the gratitude which your faithfulness and service deserve."

The whole purpose indeed of priestly formation is summarized in *faithfulness* and *service*.

XIII

Religious: Inseparable from the Church's Life and Holiness

It is a joy to reflect on *consecrated religious life* in the Church.

When we turn our thoughts to the theme of consecrated religious life in the Church we automatically think of so many religious whom we have known in our lives. To speak about religious life is to think about all the Sisters and Brothers who have taught in our schools; all the religious who have served in the healthcare ministry of our local Churches; all the religious who have given their lives in generous and selfless collaboration to help build the Kingdom of God, many of whom are in advanced age and continue to offer their lives for the Church. To speak about religious life is to think about the extraordinary activity that has been accomplished by all the religious in the Church, in the missions—the men and women religious who have left their native countries in order to go forth in the name of Jesus to help proclaim the Gospel of salvation to the ends of the earth. To speak about religious life is to remember the witness of self-sacrifice and the extraordinary testimony of joy and peace that so many men and women religious have offered to the Church and to the world. To speak about religious life is to be mindful of a debt of gratitude of which the people of God are very conscious and to which we all owe the religious of the Church.

The Second Vatican Council speaks with great love and affection about the religious of the Church. It does this both in the Dogmatic Constitution on the Church as well as in the Decree on the Adapted Renewal of Religious Life. In the Constitution on the Church, Vatican II presents every category in the Church as *part of the People of God.* The hierarchy, the laity, and the religious all make up the one People of God in which there is an interrelationship of solidarity and mutual support.

The Constitution on the Church treats religious life immediately after treating the universal call to holiness. There is a beautiful statement at the beginning of the Council's treatment of religious that is very inspirational. It says: "Although the religious state constituted by the profession of the evangelical counsels does not pertain to the hierarchical structure of the Church, nevertheless it belongs inseparably to her life and holiness" (no. 44). This tells us so much about religious life. It tells us that it is constituted by the profession of the evangelical counsels, which the Council enumerates as those of chastity, poverty, and obedience. It also tells us that religious life is bound up and so relevant to the life and holiness of the entire Church.

Consecration and Mission

The Council's basic description of religious life is very important and merits a great deal of reflection. The Council insists that *the fundamental norm of religious life is the follow-ing of Christ as proposed by the Gospel.* It characterizes this as the supreme law of religious life. The Council also goes on to say that religious life is intended, above all else, to lead those who embrace it to an imitation of Christ and to union with God through the profession of the evangelical counsels. And by the profession of evangelical counsels, the Council states that religious have answered a divine call *to live for God alone.* They have handed over their lives to God's service in an act of special *consecration,* which is deeply rooted in their baptismal consecration and which provides a fuller manifestation of it. These words truly help us to understand so many of the religious who have crossed our paths from the days of our youth—the men and women whom we remember as answering a divine call to live for God and to serve God's people.

These two elements figure greatly in the explanation of religious life, namely, *consecration* and *mission.* To fulfill both of these aspects worthily, the Council encourages religious to cultivate energetically the spirit and the practice of *prayer.*

The Decree on Religious Life dedicated its attention to the renewal of religious life, which it envisions as requiring adjustments and accommodations in the modern world. Two important principles are laid down, however, to guide the renewal of religious life according to the Council. The first is a continuous *return* to the sources of Christian life and to the original inspiration of a given community—in other words, *to the spirit of the founders or foundresses.* The second element is an *adjustment* of the community *to the changed conditions of our times.*

The ecclesial aspect of all religious communities is emphasized by the Council, when it says that *all communities should participate in the life of the Church.* This is indeed one of the elements of any adjustment that is made in religious communities. The Council also speaks about a renewal of spirit that must be coupled with the promotion of exterior works.

Demands of the Evangelical Counsels and Community Life

Vatican II spells out very clearly the demands for religious of *chastity, poverty,* and *obedience.* It is interesting to see how the Council links the evangelical counsel of chastity with the practice of fraternal love among members, citing fraternal love as a safeguard to chastity. Vatican II says that religious poverty requires more than limiting the use of possessions to the consent of superiors. It enjoins upon members of the community to be poor both in fact and spirit. Communities should aim at giving also a kind of corporate witness to poverty. And here the Council asks that communities give something from their own resources for the needs of the Church and the support of the poor whom religious should love with the tenderness of Christ. Certainly Vatican II would be in complete agreement with the desire of religious today to show special care for the poor, for all those in need, especially of justice and human dignity. There are many aspects to obedience, but all of them are a further expression of the fact that obedience entails sacrifice and a total dedication of the will of a religious. By this obedience, religious unite themselves with Jesus Himself who came to do the Father's will.

The Council speaks of the early Church as providing an *example of community life,* when the believers were of one heart and one mind and found nourishment in the teaching of the Gospel and in the Eucharist. In the community life held forth to religious they are asked to bear one another's burdens and in that way to fulfill the law of Christ. The ideal presented to the religious community is that of a true family gathered together in the name of Jesus, rejoicing in His presence and holding love as the fulfillment of the law and the bond of perfection.

How beautifully the Council links the vocation to religious life to *the holiness of the Church*. It says that through the religious life there should be a more vigorous flowering of the Church's holiness for the greater glory of the one and undivided Trinity, which in Christ and through Christ is the fountain and wellspring of all holiness.

The Council also explains the concept of what is called the "exemption" of religious life. It says that any institute of perfection can be removed from the jurisdiction of the local Ordinaries by the Holy Father and made subject only to him. It points out that this is possible by virtue of his primacy over the entire Church. This indeed is what has happened in the history of the Church. Religious have received a certain exemption from diocesan jurisdiction, as far as their religious lives go, in order to pursue their apostolates that are not directly for the benefit of an individual Church, but at the service of the universal Church. This fact highlights how much religious orders are indebted to the Holy Father, how closely they are bound to the See of Peter and how important it is that they look upon all their apostolates, all their ministries as being coordinated by the Apostolic See and being dependent on the Pope. How important, therefore, is the concept of *the unity of religious with the Holy See.* And this unity is of course expressed by their faithful obedience in the service of the Gospel, faithful obedience first of all to the Pope himself. At the same time, the Council says that the members of religious communities owe reverence and obedience to the Bishops who possess pastoral authority over the individual Churches and are called to coordinate in unity and harmony various apostolic labors.

The Council speaks about many aspects of consecrated life. It confirms the validity of those communities

that are *totally dedicated to contemplation* and that in solitude
and silence proclaim the primacy of God in the world.
It also pays homage to the venerable institution of *monastic
life*, saying that it should be faithfully preserved and it should
grow ever increasingly radiant in the life of the Church.

In addition to consecrated religious life, the Council
has authoritatively recognized *Societies of Apostolic Life*.
They are important in the life of the Church, because they
pursue a specific apostolic or missionary end. In many of
these societies, there is an explicit commitment to the evangelical counsels through sacred bonds officially recognized
by the Church. Vatican II fully accepts and approves *Secular
Institutes*, which are not religious communities, but which
profess the evangelical counsels and in which the members
live out a consecration to God that is inspired by perfect
charity. This type of ecclesial institute does not embrace
public vows or the requirement of community life, and yet
the Church recognizes this as an authorized form of the
life of evangelical perfection in the world. The recognition
of this type of life was first given under Pope Pius XII in
the Constitution *Provida Mater* of February 2, 1947. Hence,
this form of consecrated life is not religious life nor is it a
lay apostolate.

Witnesses to the Praying, Loving, and Serving Christ

The entire legacy of the Second Vatican Council as it affects
consecrated life is found in the Post-Synodal Apostolic
Exhortation *Vita Consecrata*—"Consecrated Life." This
document was published on March 25, 1996, and it codified
all the intuitions of the Church in regard to the various
forms of consecrated life. So many of the issues that are
implicit in the teaching of Vatican II become explicit in this

document on consecrated life. The relationship of consecrated life to *evangelization* is spelled out. The *preference for the poor and the promotion of justice* are splendidly set forth. The *care of the sick* is beautifully presented in its relationship to consecrated life. Consecrated men and women are reminded that they should foster respect for the human person and for human life from conception to its natural end.

It is evident from the Council's teaching on religious life, and even more from the post-synodal teaching of *Vita Consecrata*, that there are great challenges to the religious life. It is a delicate area in the life of the Church, because it concerns the pursuit of holiness. The evangelical counsels of chastity, poverty, and obedience require wisdom and generosity in their application. The people of God who need the witness of religious life and other forms of consecrated life are called to pray for religious and to express to them an affirmation in their consecration and mission that means so much to the Church. This support of the people of God is very important, because Vatican II identifies the mission of religious life as being the mission of the Church. The people of God wish to see the religious in the role that the Council presents to the Church, namely, as *witnesses to the praying, loving, and serving Christ.*

The Church on her part desires, through religious themselves, to give an increasingly clearer revelation of Christ to believers and nonbelievers alike. Just as the Council itself recognized the relationship of religious life to the Most Blessed Trinity, so also the Synod document of Pope John Paul II proclaims consecrated life as a *great gift of the Most Blessed Trinity to the Church.*

In the true spirit of Vatican II, Pope John Paul II showed a deep interest over the years in religious life in the United States. He expressed profound gratitude to the religious of the Church, highlighting the great contributions that they have made throughout the history of the United States. Back in 1983 the Holy Father wrote to the American Bishops specifically about the religious of the United States, saying: "In reflecting on their history, their splendid contribution to the Church in your country, the great missionary activity that they have performed over the years, the influence they have exerted on religious life throughout the world, as well as on the particular needs that they experience at the present time, I am convinced that, as Bishops, we must offer them encouragement and the support of our pastoral love" (Letter of April 3, 1983).

He then went on to describe how much has been done by the religious in the United States, saying: "The religious life in the United States has indeed been *a great gift of God to the Church and to your country.* From the early colonial days, by the grace of God, the evangelizing zeal of outstanding men and women religious, encouraged and sustained by the persevering efforts of the Bishops, have helped the Church to bring the fruits of the redemption to your land. Religious were among your pioneers. They blazed a trail in Catholic education at all levels, helping to create a magnificent educational system, from elementary school to university. They brought into being healthcare facilities remarkable both for their numbers and quality. They made a valuable contribution to the provision of social services. Working towards the establishment of justice, love and peace, they help to build a social order rooted in the Gospel, striving to bring generation after generation to the maturity of Christ. Their witness to the primacy of Christ's love has been expressed through lives of prayer and dedicated service to others. Contemplative religious have contributed immensely to the vitality of the ecclesial community.

At every stage in its growth, the Church in your nation, marked by a conspicuous fidelity to the See of Peter has been deeply indebted to its religious: priests, sisters, brothers. The religious of America have also been a gift to the universal Church, for they have given generously to the Church in other countries; they have helped throughout the world to evangelize the poor and to spread Christ's Gospel of peace."

The demands on religious are many. The ideals are lofty. The obstacles to authenticity are frequent, and this means that the challenges are daunting. But *the support of the Church for consecrated life,* so authoritatively expressed by Vatican II, is constant.

Awaiting the Contribution of Young Consecrated Persons

As a diocesan Bishop, one of my greatest obligations is to promote vocations to the diocesan priesthood, to provide for the needs of the local Church. But I am conscious that as a Bishop of the Church in union with the See of Peter and with the Roman Pontiff I have an obligation also to encourage young people who feel attracted to the special charisms of authentic consecrated life. In this spirit I make my own the words of Pope John Paul II in his Post-Synodal Apostolic Exhortation as he speaks to young people, saying: "To you young people I say: if you hear the Lord's call, do not reject it! Dare to become part of the great movements of holiness which renowned Saints have launched in their following of Christ. Cultivate the ideals proper to your age, but readily accept God's plan for you if he invites you to seek holiness in the consecrated life. Admire all God's works in the world, but be ready to fix your eyes on the things destined never to pass away. The third millennium awaits the contribution of the faith and creativity of great numbers of young consecrated persons, that the world may be made more peaceful and able to welcome God and in him all his sons and daughters" (*Vita Consecrata*, no. 106).

With Vatican II, the Church convincingly repeats: "Although the religious state constituted by the profession of the evangelical counsels does not belong to the hierarchical structure of the Church, nevertheless it belongs inseparably to her life and holiness."

XIV

The Laity:
Called to Sanctify the World

Back in February of 1946 Pope Pius XII gave an extraordinary talk in which he spoke of *the dignity of the laity.* His phrase at the time was "The laity are the Church." Obviously, he was not speaking in some exclusive manner. He was not saying that the laity are the Church to the exclusion of the hierarchy or religious. He was not saying that Bishops, priests, deacons, and consecrated religious are less important members of the Church. But he was insisting that the laity *are* the Church. They are the Church in the sense that they make up the Church. They not only belong to the Church, they not only serve the Church, they not only live their lives in fidelity to the teachings of the Church and receive the sacraments of the Church, but they *are* the Church. They are part of the Body of Christ in the fullest sense and they constitute an extraordinary percentage of the baptized. The Second Vatican Council fell heir to this teaching of Pius XII, which for a number of years was developing *under the inspiration of the Holy Spirit* in the Church.

As we look back on Vatican II, we can boast that one of its greatest successes, through God's grace, was a new realization by the laity of their dignity and of their mission. The Dogmatic Constitution on the Church of the Second Vatican Council emphasized *the People of God* and it showed how the hierarchy, the laity, and the religious of the Church are all part of God's people, all related to each other in the Body of Christ, which is the Church.

After presenting the overall picture of the Church as the People of God, and after having reflected on the mystery of the Church in her deep identity, at that point Vatican II presents its teaching on the laity as such. In addition to the general presentation made in the Constitution on the Church, which is called *Lumen Gentium*, Vatican II reserved a special decree for the laity. It is called the Decree on the Apostolate of the Laity. Its Latin title is *Apostolicam Actuositatem*. These two documents together present a beautiful picture of *God's plan for the laity* of His Church.

On the Frontlines of the Church's Life

The Constitution on the Church was signed on November 21, 1964, and the Decree on the Laity was signed the following year, November 18, 1965. This authoritative teaching of Vatican II was ratified once again in the life of the Church thirty-three years later, on December 30, 1988, when Pope John Paul II issued his Post-Synodal Apostolic Exhortation *Christifideles Laici*. This document represented the results of the Synod of Bishops' discussion on the Church's teaching on the laity. It was a further step in the spirit of Vatican II *to call the laity to their dignity and to their mission*, and to express the total support of the Church for the lay faithful.

It is interesting to recall that in this Post-Synodal Apostolic Exhortation on the Laity Pope John Paul II once again returns to the talk of Pope Pius XII of February 20, 1946. He cites the exact words of Pius XII: "The faithful, more precisely the lay faithful, find themselves on the front lines of the Church's life; for them the Church is the animating principle for human society. Therefore, they in particular, ought to have an ever clearer consciousness *not only of belonging to the Church but of being the Church,* that is to say, the community of the faithful on earth under the leadership of the Pope, the head of all, and of the Bishops in communion with him. These *are the Church* . . ." (no. 9).

The Council itself was greatly indebted to Pius XII. And the Synod of Bishops and the Post-Synodal Apostolic Exhortation of Pope John Paul II were deeply indebted to the Second Vatican Council. It is some of the content of the Council that I would like to share with you.

A rich doctrinal presentation of the laity constitutes chapter four of *Lumen Gentium.* Vatican II states that the Bishops of the Church know that they themselves were not meant by Christ to shoulder alone the entire saving mission of the Church. The Bishops share this with their priests and deacons. Consecrated religious are also part of this saving mission. But all the baptized are likewise needed to participate in the mission of the Church, because all the baptized "are the Church." By the term "laity," the Second Vatican Council understands all the faithful of the Church, except those in Holy Orders and those in consecrated life. The laity are the members of Christ who, by their Baptism and Confirmation, seek to build up the Kingdom of God by engaging in temporal affairs and by ordering them according to God's plan.

The laity live in the world, participate in secular professions and occupations. They live in the ordinary circumstances of family and social life in which the very web of their existence is woven. The laity are called by God *to work for the sanctification of the world from within* and in the manner of leaven. As Christ's faithful, the laity are part of the entire people of God and overwhelmingly constitute the Body of Christ.

Commissioned to Participate

The *lay apostolate* reflects the fact that the laity "are" the Church. The lay apostolate is a participation by the laity in the very saving mission of the Church. If, in the words of Pope Pius XII, "the laity are the Church," then they must be involved essentially in the mission that Christ has given to His Church. Their participation in this mission is, in the terminology of Vatican II, *the lay apostolate*. What is so exhilarating is that the Church, through Vatican II, tells the laity of the world that *it is the Lord Jesus Himself who has commissioned them to participate in the apostolate of the Church*. It is He who, through their Baptism and Confirmation, has called them to their mission.

The laity receive, through the sacraments and especially the Holy Eucharist, the strength of charity, which is the soul of their entire apostolate. In the Body of the Church the laity are called in a special way to make the Church present and active in those places and situations where their presence is so necessary. Every layperson, the Council tells us, is a witness and a living instrument of the Church's mission. The laity are *intimate collaborators with Christ* in the building up of His Body. Some of the laity, in addition to their essential role as baptized and confirmed members of the Church, dedicated to the mission of the Church, are also called to a direct form of cooperation in the apostolate of the hierarchy. This goes back a long way in the history of the Church where certain members of the laity directly collaborated with Paul the Apostle. But all the laity, and not only those chosen for a special collaboration with the hierarchy, are charged to participate in the saving work of the Church which is the work of Christ.

Vatican II goes deeply into the dignity of the laity. It explains how Christ, besides associating them with

His life and His mission, also associates them in *His priestly function of offering spiritual worship* for the glory of God and the salvation of mankind. From the very beginning it was the intention of Vatican II to show that the call to holiness of the laity is realized in their daily lives and in the context and environment in which God has placed them. And therefore all their words and prayers, their apostolic endeavors, their married and family life, their daily work, their mental and physical relaxation carried out in the Holy Spirit, and even all the sacrifices of life, if born patiently— all of these become spiritual sacrifices acceptable to God through Jesus Christ.

To Consecrate the World to God

But Vatican II says more. It says that during the celebration of the Eucharist these sacrifices that the laity make are most lovingly offered to the Father together with the Body and Blood of Christ. In this way the laity "consecrate the world itself to God." We see then that Christ associates His faithful, the laity, in His priestly activity. The laity share in the Sacrifice of Christ. Their lives are linked to His priestly oblation.

In addition to His priestly role, *Christ also shares His teaching role with the laity.* They are His witnesses in the world. The Gospel that Jesus came to proclaim shines forth in the daily, social and family life of the laity. The laity, living their lives faithfully, are heralds of faith in the future state of the Church. They evangelize with Christ and this evangelization is carried out in the ordinary and secular surroundings of the world.

In treating the laity, the Second Vatican Council obviously has a special word of support and encouragement for all those lay faithful who are sanctified by the Sacrament of Matrimony. The witness of the laity is exercised in a special way in the home, where husband and wife live their personal vocation as *witnesses of faith in Christ* to each other and to their children. The laity are always on the front lines of bringing the Gospel to the world.

In building up the Kingdom of God in a particular way, the laity are called *to relate all creation to the praise of God.* The laity must assist one another to live holier lives in the midst of their daily occupations and preoccupations. Through their activity, the world is permeated by the spirit of Christ and more effectively achieves its purpose in justice, love, and peace. Vatican II says that the laity have the principal role in this specific matter. The laity deal constantly with created goods and they are urged to work vigorously so that all created goods may be perfected for the benefit of all. Their competence in secular fields, their personal activity, their human labor all contribute to this end.

The Second Vatican Council speaks clearly about *the right of the laity* and of all Christians to receive from the Church the assistance of the word of God and the sacraments. The Bishops, Vatican II tells us, are to recognize and promote *the dignity and the responsibility of the laity* in the Church. The Bishops should willingly benefit from the prudent counsel of the laity and utilize their service to the Church. So many benefits are hoped for from an exchange that is carried out in a family spirit between laity and pastors of the Church. In this way, the laity are strengthened in their sense of personal responsibility, renewed in their enthusiasm, and more readily dedicate their talents to the work of their Bishops through a close collaboration in faith and love. The whole Church is strengthened and immensely enriched by the contribution of the laity to the mission of Christ and His Church.

The Council eloquently attests that every individual layperson must stand before the world as *a witness to the resurrection and life of the Lord Jesus and as a sign of the living God.*

In treating the Apostolate of the Laity in a separate document, the Council indicated its intention to intensify the apostolic activity of the people of God and to emphasize the indispensable role of the laity in the mission of the Church. *The apostolate of the laity,* the Council insists, *derives from their Christian vocation* and the Church can never be without it. The Council draws attention to the unmistakable work of the Holy Spirit in making the laity today ever more conscious of their responsibility and inspiring them ever more to serve Christ and the Church.

In Living Union with Christ

The Decree on the Laity very beautifully points out that *the laity,* who are incorporated into the Church through Baptism and strengthened by the power of the Holy Spirit through Confirmation, *are assigned to the apostolate by the Lord Himself.* The laity are called to share what the Council calls "the noble burden" of making God's message of salvation known and accepted throughout the world. The condition for the success of all the lay apostolate depends upon *the laity's living union with Christ.* What is so comforting for the laity in the teaching of Vatican II is that their growth in union with Christ is nourished *by active participation in the liturgy,* but it is also strengthened *by the fulfillment of their ordinary duties* in life. The words of Saint Paul are so applicable to our laity: "Whatever you do in

word or in deed, do everything in the name of the Lord
Jesus giving thanks to God the Father through him"
(Colossians 3:17).

In spelling out the goals to be achieved through
the apostolate of the laity, the Council has asserted that the
laity must take on *the renewal of the temporal order as their
own special obligation.* They are to act directly and definitively
in the temporal sphere. As citizens they must cooperate
with other citizens in renewing the temporal order. How
greatly is the contribution of the laity needed in works of
charity and projects of social assistance, including international programs in which effective help is given to needy
individuals and persons.

In presenting the various fields of the apostolate,
Vatican II has highlighted *the apostolate of married persons
and of families* and has indicated its unique importance for
the Church and civil society. Christian husbands and wives
are cooperators in grace and witnesses of faith on behalf
of each other, their children, and others in their household.
The family has received from God its mission to be the
first and vital cell of society.

Vatican II looks to families for immense help in so
many projects: the adoption of abandoned infants, hospitality
to strangers, assistance in operating schools, counsel and
help for adolescents, help for engaged couples in preparing
for marriage, catechetical work, support of married couples
and families involved in material and moral crises, and help
for the aged.

The Council has not forgotten *the apostolate of young
people* and the great influence they exert on modern society.
This particular area has been so developed by Pope John
Paul II. In every country of the world he called young
people to responsibility and to the understanding of their

mission. Vatican II has called upon children to engage in apostolic work and to be living witnesses to Christ among their companions.

In the vast fields of national and international activity, the Council calls upon the laity to be stewards of Christian wisdom. The laity are invited to promote the irresistibly increasing sense of solidarity among all peoples, which the Decree on the Lay Apostolate calls one of "the signs of our times."

Together in the Whole Church, with Joy and Zeal

The lay apostolate, whether it is exercised by individuals, organizations, or movements, should always be incorporated into *the apostolate of the whole Church* according, as the Council tells us, to a right system of relationships. Various projects of the apostolate need to be suitably coordinated by the hierarchy. Unity and fraternal charity must be resplendent in the entire apostolate of the Church.

Vatican II has turned its attention in the last chapter of the Decree on the Lay Apostolate to the question of *formation for the apostolate.* It says that, since the laity share in their own way in the mission of the Church, their apostolic formation must be imbued with its own form of spirituality. The question of the formation of the laity is an ongoing challenge to the entire Church. The Second Vatican Council specifies that, in addition to spiritual formation, there is needed solid doctrinal instruction, theology, ethics, and philosophy—instruction that is adapted to differences of age, status, and natural talents. There is a need for imparting general culture along with practical and technical training.

All of this we can see is immensely challenging. And the Council spreads it out throughout the entire Church. It talks about the training for the apostolate as starting with *a child's earliest education*. Schools—colleges and other educational institutions—have the duty to develop a Catholic sense and apostolic activity in *young people*.

Lay groups and associations should assist in promoting the formation for the apostolate. Individuals are called upon to take pains to prepare themselves personally for the apostolate. The laity are called upon to learn the principles of the social doctrine of the Church. Study sessions, congresses, periods of recollection, spiritual exercises, and other means are listed by the Council in the formidable challenge of making proper formation available. This extraordinary work must go on serenely, with joy and zeal, and always with the intention of helping the laity in the Church to fulfill the role to which they have been commissioned personally by Christ and which is *their collaboration in the mission of salvation*.

We can see then that Pope Pius XII was right. The laity are indeed the Church, not that they only belong to the Church or work for the Church or serve the Church, but they are so intimately a part of the constitution and essence of the Church, living members of the Body of Christ.

XV

The Missionary Activity of the Church: Christ's Mission Prolonged, the Plan of God Fulfilled

On October 16, 1978, I had the great privilege of standing on the balcony of the Secretariat of State, which is to the right of St. Peter's Basilica as you face it. It was from this balcony that Monsignor, now Cardinal, Giovanni Battista Re and I heard the announcement that Cardinal Karol Wojtyla, Archbishop of Krakow, had been elected Pope John Paul II. For the first time in over four hundred and fifty years, a non-Italian had been elected Bishop of Rome, Successor of Peter, and Visible Head of the universal Church. Some time after the announcement was made, the Cardinals started to leave, one by one, the Apostolic Palace. Pope John Paul II remained.

Monsignor Re and I left the balcony and walked through the Apostolic Palace. At a given moment, we met up with someone whom we both esteemed greatly, because we had worked with him and for him for a number of years. It was Cardinal Giovanni Battista Benelli, the Archbishop of Florence. He had been rumored as a candidate for the papacy. Obviously, God had other plans. It was a great joy to greet Cardinal Benelli at this moment. He was in a hurry, eager to get back to Florence, to his Archdiocese.

He would be coming back to Rome, of course, a few days later, for the solemn inauguration of the new pontificate.

"No Foreigners in the Church"

After greeting Cardinal Benelli, Monsignor Re had urgent business in his office. I was free and accompanied the Cardinal out through the Cortile San Damaso, one of the inner courtyards of the Vatican, and down into the large Cortile Belvedere where his car was parked. Right outside of Cortile San Damaso, the Cardinal was met by the press. One member of the media approached Cardinal Benelli and said to him: "Your Eminence, what do you think of the fact that a foreigner has been elected Pope?" I will never forget his reaction. Without even stopping, the Cardinal responded decisively, saying: "There are no foreigners in the Church." John Paul II from Poland was not a foreigner in Rome or in the Catholic Church. No one is.

Before His Ascension into heaven, Jesus spoke to the Apostles, saying: "You will receive power when the Holy Spirit comes upon you, and you will be my witnesses in Jerusalem, throughout Judea and Samaria, and to the ends of the earth" (Acts 1:8).

That's how it all started. The Apostles were charged to proclaim the Gospel in Jerusalem, throughout all Judea into Samaria, and, from there, to the ends of the earth.

The Apostles were the first missionaries. And all of us have inherited the faith from them, through one dimension or another of the missionary activity of the Church.

The United States is grateful to the first missionaries who, in fidelity to the command of Christ, came to this country in order to bring the Gospel. The United States is grateful to all the immigrants, all the different nations of the world who themselves had received the faith through missionaries and in the United States were able to share that faith with new generations.

To All Nations

The Decree on the Missionary Activity of the Church opens up with a brief introduction, followed by six chapters. In the brief introduction we read that the Church has been divinely sent to all nations, that she might be the universal sacrament of salvation. Jesus told the Apostles: "Go into the whole world and proclaim the Gospel to every creature. Whoever believes and is baptized will be saved; whoever does not believe will be condemned" (Mark 16:15–16).

The Church, then, is *the community of those who believe in Christ,* the community in which those who accept the teaching of Christ—those who believe—are, according to the words of Jesus, to be saved. The Decree on the Missions, called *Ad Gentes,* situates the Church in God's plan, saying: "It has not pleased God to call people to share his life merely as individuals without any mutual bonds. Rather, he wills to mold them into a people in which his children, once scattered abroad, can be gathered together" (no. 2). For this reason, the Apostles, in fidelity to the mandate of Christ, went out into the whole world. They preached the Gospel and they established the community of the Church, gathering the people together in the name of Jesus, so that everyone might receive salvation from Him.

Jesus was sent by His Father into the world to accomplish His mission of salvation, to reveal the Father's love. Just as Jesus was sent by the Father, so, in the power of the Holy Spirit, He sent the Apostles, so that His work, His mission, might be carried on to the ends of the earth and until the end of time.

Throughout the ages, the Holy Spirit unites the Church in the unity of communion and service. The Apostles were faithful to Christ's mandate and they established *successors* down throughout the ages. And, under the guidance of the Successors of the Apostles, generations of missionaries have been faithful to the words of Jesus: "Go, therefore, and make disciples of all nations, baptizing them in the name of the Father and of the Son and of the Holy Spirit, teaching them to observe all that I have commanded you. And behold, I am with you always, until the end of the age" (Matthew 28:19–20).

Today, the missionary work of the Church goes on. The mandate has to be constantly fulfilled, and the Church undertakes the missionary activity in obedience to Christ's command and in the power of the Holy Spirit.

The Second Vatican Council pointed out to us many things about the missionary activity of the Church. It mentioned that "the specific purpose of missionary activity is evangelization and the planting of the Church among those peoples and groups where she has not yet taken root" (no. 6).

The word "missions" is the term that is usually given to those particular initiatives by which heralds of the Gospel are sent out into the whole world to carry on the task of preaching the Gospel and planting the Church. Missionary activity usually refers to the activity exercised in certain territories recognized by the Holy See. We call these "mission territories," "mission countries," or "mission lands." They can be any place where the Gospel of Christ still needs to be preached and the Church planted.

In a restricted way, we speak about *the home missions.* It has a different geographical concept, but the idea is always related to Christ's mandate: "Go, make disciples of all nations, baptizing them in the name of the Father and of the Son and of the Holy Spirit."

The Church's Inmost Missionary Nature

Missionary activity in the Church *has various stages.* Sometimes these stages are found side by side. There is the beginning or the planting of the Church. Then there is the phase of newness or youth. After that, there is the continuation by the missionary Church itself, of missionary activity in sending forth missionaries to other lands. In all of this, we see that *missionary activity springs from the Church's inmost nature.*

Missionary activity is always outgoing. And the missionary activity among the nations differs from the pastoral activity exercised among the faithful in Churches long since established. Yet the common denominator in all of this is the preaching of the Gospel, evangelization, proclaiming Jesus Christ, and the establishing His Church.

Through missionary activity, the plan of God is fulfilled and *Christ's mission is prolonged.* According to this plan, the whole human race is meant to form one people of God and to come together into the one and only Body of Christ, and to be built up into the one temple of the Holy Spirit.

Christ and the Church, which bears witness to Christ by preaching the Gospel to every nation, transcend every particularity of race or nation. And the Church cannot be considered foreign anywhere or to anybody. Cardinal Benelli was right: "There are no foreigners in the Church."

Missionary activity fulfills God's will in the world and in world history. By the preaching of the word and by the celebration of the sacraments, whose center and summit is the Holy Eucharist, the missionary activity brings Christ Himself, the author of salvation, to peoples everywhere.

These principles are the doctrinal principles of the first chapter of the Decree on the Missionary Activity of the Church. And all of them presume what the Decree says explicitly: "The pilgrim Church is missionary by her very nature" (no. 2).

The Mystery of Christ Shining Forth

The Church takes her origin from the mission of the Son of God and the mission of the Holy Spirit, in accordance with the decree of God the Father. And, for the glory of the Most Blessed Trinity, the Church continues the mission of Jesus in the power of the Holy Spirit.

Chapter two speaks about the mission work itself. Even as the Church sets out to reveal and communicate the love of God to all peoples and all nations, she is aware that her missionary task is a gigantic one. There are many groups to which the Gospel must be presented. To all of them, it is presented to be accepted freely.

A great deal of the missionary activity of the Church is accomplished by the Christian witness of her members. The members of the Church are urged to share in the cultural and social life of the people with whom they live. They are urged to enter into patient dialogue with those to whom they are sent, showing always respect and charity toward those with whom they live and with whom they work in the affairs of economic and social life. They are urged to collaborate in the strivings of peoples in the struggle against famine, ignorance, and disease. Through the disciples of Christ, the mystery of Christ begins to shine forth in the world. And, through the life of Christ's followers, the love of God is revealed. This too is an important part of missionary activity.

Missionary activity requires the preaching of the Gospel, the communication of Christ. The Council tells us that those who have accepted faith in Christ should be admitted to the catechumenate through liturgical rites. The catechumenate is an apprenticeship of appropriate length in which the catechumens are properly instructed in the mystery of salvation and the practice of Gospel morality. The Church strictly forbids forcing anyone to embrace the faith, or alluring or enticing people by unworthy methods. She also insists on a person's right to embrace the faith and not to be deterred from it by unjust vexation. *The Holy Spirit, in all evangelization, is the principal agent.* It is He who calls people to Christ by the seed of God's word and by the preaching of the Gospel. It is He who stirs up in their hearts the obedience of faith.

The missionaries in the history of the Church have been admirably assisted by *the catechists.* The Second Vatican Council expressed a deep debt of gratitude to the catechists of the Church. These are men and women who, side by side with the missionaries, have helped present the Gospel message to the people of their community. Sometimes the catechists of mission lands have lived and worked as heroes of the faith, ensuring the survival of the Church, when Bishops and priests were no longer permitted to function.

I remember some years back when I was able to be present with Pope John Paul II in the small African nation of Equatorial Guinea. This nation had suffered from tyranny. The Bishops and priests had been persecuted and decimated and yet, through the work of catechists, the life of the community went on. Equatorial Guinea had been a Spanish possession at one time and Spanish is still spoken there to some extent. I remember an old man, on the occasion of the Pope's visit, coming up to me. He was barefoot but he wore a papal medal that had been given to him in recognition of his distinguished service to the Church. He smiled and told me that he was a catechist: *"Yo soy catequista."* I immediately understood what that meant in the context of Equatorial Guinea. He was one of the heroes who had helped, despite the persecution, to maintain the faith. He had catechized and transmitted the faith in spite of all the opposition and tyranny that had been unleashed against the Church.

Missionary Activity, Prayer, Sacrifice, and Conversion of Heart

In chapter four the Council extols *the missionary vocation.* Missionaries are sent by the Church to proclaim the Gospel in foreign lands. The Council speaks about the requirements of the missionary role. It speaks to us about the necessary preparation for the missionary task. It has never been easy and it never will be. But anyone, the Council says, who is going to encounter another people should have a great esteem for their patrimony, their language, and their customs. It is only then that the missionary can effectively present Christ.

The Decree on the Missions also speaks about *the organization of missionary activity* and about *missionary responsibility.* The Bishops of the Church, as the Successors of the Apostles, obviously have the primary responsibility to see that the mandate of Christ is carried out. The Holy See has established an effective organization called the Congregation for the Evangelization of Peoples, once also called *De Propaganda Fide* or the Propagation of Faith. To a great extent it coordinates the missionary activity of the Church. In individual dioceses there is an office for this purpose that collaborates in the missionary activity of the universal Church. The missionary generosity of the people of the United States has been great and the challenges will continue for years to come.

The concluding chapter on the Decree of the Missionary Activity of the Church states that "since the whole Church is missionary and the work of evangelization is a basic duty of the people of God, this Ecumenical Council summons everyone to a deep interior renewal" (no. 35). The Church is saying, in effect, what she has always said: There is a connection between missionary activity and prayer and sacrifice and conversion of heart. It is for this reason that Saint Thérèse of Lisieux can today be recognized as the co-patron of the missions, not because she ever stepped foot on missionary territory, but because she lived a life of holiness and prayer, of deep interior renewal.

The Council shows its true colors when it proclaims: "Let all realize that their first and most important obligation toward the spread of the faith is this: to lead a profoundly Christian life" (no. 36). And the Council went on to say that the fervor of the faithful, their service of God and their charity toward others would cause new spiritual inspiration to sweep over the whole Church. Then she will appear as a sign lifted up among the nation, "the light of the world" and "the salt of the earth."

Vatican II draws attention to the obligation of the Bishop to promote the work of the missions and to show *missionary spirit and zeal* so that the whole diocese becomes missionary. But it is also the Bishop's task to look to the sick and those suffering hardship to find souls who will offer prayer and penance to God with a generous heart for the evangelization of the world.

The Council is proud to underline *the role of prayer, penance, and suffering* that contemplative communities exercise for the conversion of souls. It reminds us that God sends workers into His harvest when, according to the Gospel, He is asked to do so.

Religious communities dedicated to the active life, whether they pursue a strictly mission goal or not, are requested by the Council to ask themselves in the presence of God whether they cannot broaden their activity in favor of expanding God's kingdom among the nations. The Council goes on even to suggest that they might consider leaving certain ministries to others, so that they themselves can spend their energies on the missions. They are asked if they can undertake work among the missions, even adapting their Constitutions if necessary. They are further asked whether their members are involved as much as possible in missionary activity and whether their type of life bears a Gospel witness that is accommodated to the character and condition of the people. Priests and laypeople are similarly challenged to take on a missionary mentality.

The final words of the Decree on the Missionary Activity of the Church express confidence in the intercession of the Virgin Mary, Queen of the Apostles, in order that the nations might be led to Christ.

And the very last phrase summarizes so much of missionary activity, because it acknowledges that everything is done through *the Holy Spirit.* He is *the supreme agent of all evangelization, of all missionary activity,* past, present, and future.

XVI

Christian Education:
Communicating Christ

The Church in the United States can be justly proud of *the long tradition of Catholic education* that exists in this land. It is a tradition that reflects a marvelous measure of commitment on the part of the people of God, and it represents a characteristic of the evangelization that has been carried on with great success by the Church in the United States. To recognize this achievement is not an expression of triumphalism. It is a duty to admire how God's graces work in the history of our people.

It is normal, therefore, that the Church in the United States would have a great interest in what the Second Vatican Council said to the world about Christian education in its Decree entitled *Gravissimum Educationis*. Vatican II has spelled out very clearly what it considers the aims of Christian education. It states: "Christian education . . . aims above all at ensuring that the baptized, as they are gradually introduced into the mystery of salvation may grow ever more conscious of the gift of faith which they have received; that they may learn to adore God the Father in spirit and in truth (cf. John 4:23), especially through liturgical worship; and that they may be prepared to lead their personal lives according to a new nature, in justice and holiness of truth (Ephesians 4:22–24); so that they may reach perfect maturity, in the measure of the fullness of Christ (cf. Ephesians 4:13) and make their contribution to the increase of the Mystical Body" (*Gravissimum Educationis,* no. 2).

Precisely because of the nature of Christian education, the Council reminds the Bishops of their duty to make every effort to see that all the faithful enjoy this education, especially the young people who are the hope of the Church. The Council draws attention to the obligation of *parents* to educate their children and at the same time it acknowledges them as the first and foremost educators of their children. The Council emphasizes how suitable *the family* is for promoting education. While belonging primarily to the family, the task of imparting education requires the help of *society* as a whole. Society shares responsibility for the education of children. It is in this context that the Council invokes the principle of subsidiarity, leaving to society the completion of the task of education according to parental directives.

Enlivened By the Gospel Spirit of Freedom and Charity

The Council recognizes that education belongs, by a unique title, to *the Church* that has the responsibility of proclaiming salvation to all and of communicating the life of Christ to those who believe. As a mother, the Church, Vatican II tells us, is bound to give her children the kind of education through which *their entire lives can be penetrated with the spirit of Christ.* And at the same time the Church promotes, through education, the full development of the human person for the well-being of society and for building a world that is more human. The Church is interested in every aspect of education, but certainly catechetical training is foremost in her plan.

Vatican II recognizes that among all the agencies of education *the school* has a special importance. The school is able to foster between students of diverse temperament and background a willingness to understand one another. Vatican II expresses esteem and admiration for those who assist parents in their task of education by undertaking *the role of teacher*. Parents are recognized as having the first and the inalienable duty and right to educate their children. And with this right and duty they should enjoy true freedom in the choice of schools.

The Council speaks to the question of *public authority* in its obligation to defend the liberty of citizens in the matter of education. The State is obliged, in the teaching of Vatican II, to protect the right of children to receive an adequate schooling. The State should be vigilant about the ability of teachers and the quality of their training. It should look after the health of students. The State must keep in mind the principle of subsidiarity so that no school monopoly arises. The Church is keenly aware of her own serious obligation to give zealous attention to the moral and religious education of all of her children. She feels a need to help those children who are trained outside of Catholic schools. In the United States, the parish school of religion has been given great attention and requires even greater attention before the immense challenges that still exist.

The Council is very conscious of the contribution of *the Catholic school*, which pursues cultural growth and the natural development of youth. Just like other schools the Catholic school pursues cultural goals and natural development of youth. In addition, it aims at creating a school community in an atmosphere enlivened by the Gospel spirit of freedom and charity. The Council says explicitly that the Catholic school retains its immense importance in the circumstances of our times. The Council likewise proclaims the Church's right to establish and to run schools of every kind and at every level.

To Give Witness to Christ

The Decree on Education calls upon *teachers to realize how important they are* in determining whether the Catholic school can effectively fulfill its goals. Teachers need to be enriched by both secular and religious knowledge and be appropriately certified. They are called upon to be imbued by an apostolic spirit and *to give witness to Christ,* the unique teacher, by their lives and by their teaching. Teachers perform their services as *partners of parents.* The Council does not hesitate to assert that the service of worthy teachers is a true apostolate and renders authentic service to society.

The Council calls upon Catholic parents to entrust their children to Catholic schools, when and where this is possible, and to support these Catholic schools to the extent of their ability.

Mention is made of schools for particular purposes and for *persons requiring special care,* as well as of schools preparing teachers to give religious instruction and other types of education. An appeal is made to the faithful for sacrifice in helping Catholic schools achieve their purpose and to show special concern for the needs of the poor and the deprived.

Vatican II insists on the importance of *Catholic higher learning,* especially colleges and universities and their faculties. The Council expresses a commitment to due freedom of scientific investigation and to show how faith and reason give harmonious witness to the unity of all truth. The Church expresses the hope that the students of

institutions of higher learning may become people of outstanding learning, able to witness the faith to the world.

The Council recommends to the attention of Bishops
the need for *Catholic residences and centers* at colleges and
universities that are not Catholic. The Council asks ecclesiastical faculties zealously to promote the sacred sciences.
Every effort should be made for collaboration between
various Catholic schools in collaboration between Catholic
schools and other schools, always with a view toward the
well-being of the whole human family.

The Council concludes by exhorting young people
to be aware of *the excellence of the teaching vocation,* to be
ready to undertake it with a generous spirit, especially where
a shortage of teachers is causing a crisis in the training of
the young. Vatican II expresses profound gratitude toward
all those who, with evangelical self-dedication, devote
themselves to the excellent work of education at every level.
It exhorts them to excel, in imbuing their students with the
spirit of Christ, in the art of teaching and in the advance-
ment of knowledge.

The Church Is Deeply Grateful

Some fourteen years after the promulgation of this Decree,
at the beginning of his pontificate, Pope John Paul II sent
a filmed message to the National Catholic Educational
Association of the United States. In this message, he summarized much of what was contained in the conciliar document. He sent a message of encouragement and blessing
to all the assembled educators, confirming them in their
important role as Catholic educators. He spoke these words:
"The Holy Spirit is with you and the Church is deeply
grateful for your dedication. The Pope speaks to you in

order to confirm you in your lofty role as Catholic educators, to assist you, to direct you, *to support you.*

"Among the many reflections that could be made at this time there are three points in particular to which I would like to make a brief reference at the beginning of my pontificate. These are: *the value of Catholic schools, the importance of Catholic teachers* and educators, and *the nature of Catholic education itself.* These are themes that have been developed at length by my predecessors. At this time, however, it is important that I add my own testimony to theirs, in the special hope of giving a *new impulse to Catholic education* throughout the vast area of the United States of America.

"With profound conviction I ratify and reaffirm the words that Paul VI spoke originally to the Bishops of your country: 'Brethren, we know the difficulties involved in preserving Catholic schools, and the uncertainties of the future, and yet we rely on the help of God and on your own zealous collaboration and untiring efforts, so that Catholic schools can continue, despite grave obstacles, to fulfill their providential role at the service of genuine Catholic education, and at the service of your country' (Address of September 15, 1975). Yes, the Catholic school must remain *a privileged means of Catholic education in America.* As an instrument of the apostolate, it is worthy of the greatest sacrifices.

"But no Catholic school can be effective without dedicated Catholic teachers, convinced of the great ideal of Catholic education. The Church needs men and women who are intent on teaching by word and example—intent on helping to permeate the whole education milieu with the spirit of Christ. *This is a great vocation,* and the Lord Himself will reward all who serve in it as educators in the cause of the word of God.

"In order that the Catholic school and the Catholic teachers may truly make their irreplaceable contribution to the Church and to the world, the goal of Catholic education itself must be crystal clear. Beloved sons and daughters of the Catholic Church, brothers and sisters in the faith: *Catholic education is above all a question of communicating Christ,* of helping to form Christ in the lives of others. In the expression of the Second Vatican Council, those who have been baptized must be made ever more aware of the gift of faith that they have received, they must learn to adore the Father in spirit and in truth, and they must be trained to live the newness of Christian life in justice and in the holiness of truth (cf. *Gravissimum Educationis,* no. 2).

"These are indeed essential aims of Catholic education. To foster and promote them gives meaning to the Catholic school; it spells out the dignity of the vocation of Catholic education.

"Yes, it is above all a question of communicating Christ, and helping His uplifting Gospel to take root in the hearts of the faithful. Be strong, therefore, in pursuing these goals. *The cause of Catholic education is the cause of Jesus Christ and of His Gospel at the service of man.*

"And be assured of the solidarity of the entire Church, and of the sustaining grace of our Lord Jesus Christ" (Filmed Address of April 1979).

In his service to the Church in the United States, Pope John Paul II kept alive the important teaching of the Council on Christian education. It is important for the Church in our country that the inspiration of Vatican II continue to direct all efforts of Catholic education in our country for years to come.

Epilogue

At the end of our reflections on the various documents of the Second Vatican Council, we are more than ever convinced that Vatican II is all about Jesus Christ.

At this moment, we hear again those words recorded in the Gospel of Saint John—that some Greeks addressed to the apostle Philip: "We would like to see Jesus" (John 12:21). We know that our challenge as Christian people is indeed to show Jesus to the world. The accomplishment of this mission is linked to our personal witness to the Lord, but it also involves transmitting to others the legacy of Catholic faith, which is Vatican II.

Our prayerful meditation on the content of this Council and our personal commitment to its authentic implementation under the guidance of Pope Benedict XVI and the Bishops of the Church are a worthy response to a great outpouring of the Holy Spirit. Through Vatican II the Holy Spirit has indeed made it possible for so many people "to see Jesus."